Families in conflict

Perspectives of children and parents on the Family Court Welfare Service

Ann Buchanan, Joan Hunt, Harriet Bretherton and Victoria Bream

The Policy
P ~ P
P R E S S

The
Nuffield
Foundation

First published in Great Britain in November 2001 by

The Policy Press
34 Tyndall's Park Road
Bristol BS8 1PY
UK

Tel +44 (0)117 954 6800
Fax +44 (0)117 973 7308
e-mail tpp@bristol.ac.uk
www.policypress.org.uk

British Library Cataloguing in Publication Data

A catalogue record for this book is available from the British Library

ISBN 1 86134 333 7

Ann Buchanan is Reader in Social Work, **Joan Hunt** is Senior Research Fellow, **Harriet Bretherton** is Research Associate and **Victoria Bream** is Research Officer, all in the Department of Social Policy and Social Work, University of Oxford, UK.

Cover design by Qube Design Associates, Bristol.

Printed and bound in Great Britain by Hobbs the Printers Ltd, Southampton.

Contents

List of figures and tables

Figures

Tables

Foreword

Over the years since the implementation of the 1989 Children Act the welfare of the child during family conflict has moved to centre stage. This research study gives a comprehensive picture of the state of the Family Court Welfare Service and the views of the people that really matter: children and their parents. This sort of information is especially important to the Children and Family Court Advisory and Support Service (CAFCASS) because every day our staff work with children who are probably facing the most difficult and emotional time of their childhood.

This report shows that children and families need more support throughout the whole process, and more information about the judicial process. It reminds us of the vital need to be more open to diversity and disadvantage and to serve everyone according to their individual needs. It demonstrates the need to train CAFCASS staff to deal more effectively with domestic violence. Most important of all it implores us to involve children in every step of the way.

All of these observations strike at the heart of our vision at CAFCASS. Our team will work tirelessly to represent the voice of the child so that changes required in social policy to bring about sustainable and tangible improvements in the lives of the many vulnerable children and families we serve really does take place at the earliest practicable opportunity.

Anthony Hewson OBE
CAFCASS

Acknowledgements

Our thanks go first and foremost to the parents and children who agreed to take part in this study. The parents shared what were often painful feelings about a process that had touched them and their family deeply. They also contributed their ideas about how the process could be changed for the better for children and parents in the future. We are particularly grateful to the parents who gave permission for their children to be interviewed.

We thank the children for their willingness to talk about events and feelings that had often been distressing for them. They provided a unique insight into how private law family proceedings are experienced by the children whose 'best interests' these proceedings are designed to promote.

The study would not have been possible without the positive support of the three Family Court Welfare Services: senior management gave permission for the study to take place in their area; the Senior Family Court Welfare Officers enthusiastically supported the research in each team; the Family Court Welfare Officers promoted the study with the parents they saw and the administrative staff took on the additional task of seeking the permission of parents and referring on to the research team.

We are grateful to the Nuffield Foundation, which funded the research, and particularly to Sharon Witherspoon who gave invaluable advice and support throughout. The Advisory Group gave us the benefit of their wide-ranging experience and knowledge, providing constructive criticism and encouragement throughout. Special thanks are owed to Gillian Douglas who acted as our consultant. Thanks are also due to the Lord Chancellor's Department, which gave permission for the study to be carried out and provided a representative to sit on our Advisory Group. Our thanks also go to Mrs C. Burry of the Records Management Services in the Lord Chancellor's Department for checking the typescript in record time.

Eirini Flouri, from the University of Oxford, gave generously of her time and patience explaining the mysteries of SPSS and statistical imperatives. And last, but far from least, we each have family, friends and professional colleagues whom we would like to thank for their wisdom, their encouragement and their divergent thinking and who need to be acknowledged even though they are too many to be named.

Membership of the Advisory Group

Professor Gillian Douglas (University of Cardiff)
Francis Flaxington (HM Inspector of Probation)
Eunice Halliday (National Association of Child Contact Centres)
Professor Adrian James (University of Bradford)
Tony Jeeves (Lord Chancellor's Department)
Peter Jeffries (Inner London Probation Service)
Judge Michael Payne
Dr Martin Richards (University of Cambridge)
Sharon Witherspoon (Nuffield Foundation)

Research team

Dr Ann Buchanan
Joan Hunt
Harriet Bretherton
Victoria Bream

Current issues and concerns

When marriages cannot be saved, government should ensure that the divorce process does not make it worse. (Home Office, 1998, Section 4.41)

The parents and children in this study give voice to some of the most profound debates within our society. When parents separate, should one parent take a leading role in making decisions about and caring for the children or should both parents have equal, even if not identical, responsibilities? What rights and responsibilities are implied by a biological relationship to a child? Does a biological tie entitle a parent to an ongoing relationship with their child or does the role of parent have to be earned? How should disputes about the arrangements for children on separation be resolved? What part should children play in decisions about their own lives?

When families are together, parents make decisions within the family about the definition, sharing and division of parenting roles. Couples make very different decisions depending on their own individual personalities, their background, their economic situation and the resources available to them in the extended family and their local community. The state will only be involved at the margins in providing some care outside the immediate family through nurseries and schools.

When parents separate the disagreements of individual couples about the definition and division of parental roles may become public and the state then becomes the arbitrator. Courts are called on to intervene in the most intimate of relationships between children and their parents. Courts rely heavily on welfare reports, prepared by Children and Family Reporters when deciding what is in the best interests of the children.

Parental separation almost inevitably involves a degree of conflict. However, for the parents in the study the level of conflict was likely to be particularly high. They had, by definition, been unable to reach a decision about the arrangements for the children between themselves. How well equipped were the courts to make decisions where parental conflict was a major factor? How did the children react to the conflict itself and the court decision-making process? What happened after the court made its decision?

This study sought to find out from children and parents what it felt like for the courts, and more particularly a Family Court Welfare Officer (FCWO)[1], to be involved in making decisions about their family life and how they saw those decisions affecting their relationships. Did they believe that the decisions made and the processes involved were appropriate, and did the arrangements made remain relevant as circumstances changed?

This report is essentially a consumer report. One hundred separated parents (in 73 cases with 116 children involved in proceedings) who had not been able to agree the arrangements for their children gave us their views on how they perceived the process of welfare reporting and the court's involvement in their disputes. Parents were interviewed just after the end of their judicial proceedings and then again a year later. At this time 30 children were also interviewed. (See Appendix A for the full methodology.)

Changing families

In the last 30 years, social changes have challenged traditional views about family life (Buchanan and Ten Brinke, 1997):

- Marriage rates have reached their lowest point since records began more than 150 years ago.
- Cohabitation has increased in a quarter of a century from being the experience of 6% to 60% of brides before their wedding day.
- Nearly one in three births occur outside marriage compared to one in sixteen 30 years ago.
- There are fewer large families; fertility rates have declined from 2.9 children per woman in 1964 to 1.8.
- Although the current divorce rate is now stable, the annual divorce rate is six-fold greater than it was in 1961. Currently four out of ten new marriages will end in divorce.
- More than one in five families with dependent children are headed by a lone parent, compared to one in twelve in 1971. The proportion of families headed by never-married single mothers has grown from 1% to 7%.
- One in twelve dependent children (8%) are living in stepfamilies. By age 16 about 6% of children will have lived in married-couple stepfamilies and 7% in cohabiting-couple stepfamilies.

Figure 1.1 (opposite) gives an overview of how these changes affect children.

Changing attitudes to family life and the role of fathers

With changing families have come more flexible attitudes to cohabitation, single and lone parenthood, divorce, working patterns and family responsibilities (Wiggins and Bynner, 1993; Halpern, 1995; Ferri and Smith, 1996).

Central to the debate is the role of fathers. While on the one hand both men and women feel that fathers should be involved in caring for children from an early age (Scott et al, 1998), fathers are being increasingly marginalised by family change. Although living with children does not ensure a father's positive involvement with them, involvement is considerably more problematic when fathers are non-resident.

Some researchers maintain that fathers only play a peripheral role in their children's lives beyond their economic contribution (Crockett et al, 1993), but there is growing evidence that intact families, in which fathers are actively 'involved', are associated with better educational, psychological and social adjustments for

their children (Lamb, 1986; Amato and Gilbreth 1999). Post-divorce the picture is more complex. The extent to which father involvement will impact on child adjustment after divorce appears to be complexly linked to the degree of conflict, type of paternal involvement and maternal acceptance, as well as the regular payment of child support (Kelly, 2000).

New knowledge on the process of divorce

Much of the earlier research assumed that divorce was an *event* leading to a short-term crisis for parents and children and a short-term 'transitional period' (Wallerstein and Kelly, 1980). As divorce became more common, further evidence from the US and the UK, particularly from the longitudinal studies (Rogers and Pryor, 1998), demonstrated that divorce was a process involving a number of factors influencing outcomes for parents and children. In this process children could move between different family forms (for example, natural family, one-parent family, stepfamily) and, for some, there would be multiple transitions. Although much of the new research focuses on divorce, the trauma following separation of established cohabiting parents, for both them and their children, may mirror that of a divorcing couple. In the short term after divorce or family disruption, most family members will experience emotional distress and difficulties (Richards and Dyson, 1982), while for some conflict may become severe or chronic.

War is not too strong a metaphor to apply to the experiences of some who divorce.... In a culture wedded to the ideal of life-long monogamy there are few social indications of how to behave, and to whom to turn, when marriage comes to an end. The resulting sense of disorientation constitutes a no-man's land in the sense that men and women are vulnerable to self-doubt, feelings of purposelessness, illness, hardship, isolation, and censure ... but the image of no-man's land can also be a hopeful one. It is the ground between opposing factions which, if they have the courage to occupy it, allows for a different relationship between those who have formally been in opposition.... Divorce is not simply a private transaction, but a legal and social act ... the interaction of those inside and outside the family during the process of divorce may generate behaviour which neither side would condone in ordinary circumstances. (Clulow and Vincent, 1987, pp 1-3)

Figure 1.1: Children in England and Wales

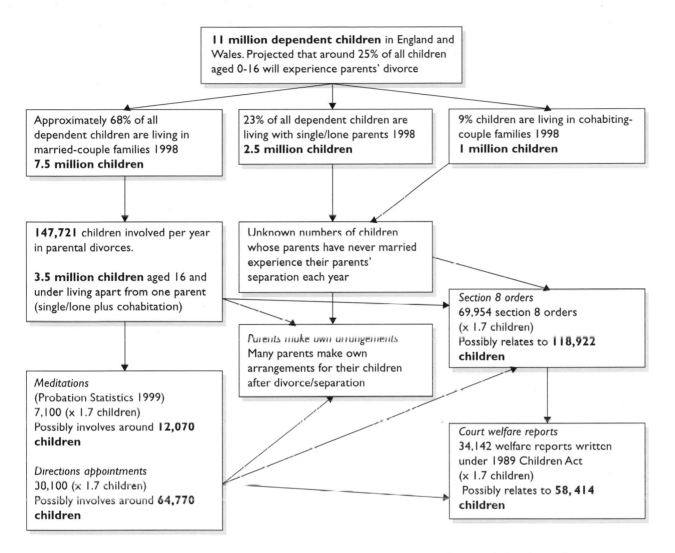

Note: Figures for couples are multiplied by 1.7 – the average number of children per couple – to calculate figures for children.

Sources: LCD (2000a, 2000b). Thanks to John Haskey and David Coleman for their assistance with these statistics.

During the process of adjustment, children need considerable support. Parental separation, however, may mean that parents are, at least for a time, less available to their children, both physically and emotionally, and communication may become stressed. Those with childcare responsibilities may have to take a full-time job because with the separation comes the likelihood of economic hardship. Weiss (1984) found that after divorce, children and families were, on average, living on half the level of income of intact families.

In a review bringing together the findings of 92 studies, Amato and Keith (1991) found that the net impact of parental divorce on children's well-being was determined by the following factors: school achievement, conduct, psychological adjustment, self-concept, social adjustment, mother–child relations and father–child relations. For children, parental separation involves both *relational* and *structural* changes. Structural changes may involve a loss in the child's *social capital* – that is, the resources he or she can draw on as they grow older (Maclean and Eekelaar, 1997). Some of the key findings from research are summarised overleaf.

Children's responses following family disruption

Very young children aged 0-4
May show separation anxieties, whining, tearful and aggressive behaviour with perhaps regression in toilet training and sleep patterns.

School-age children aged 5-8
May demonstrate anxiety, aggression and sadness, as well as a wish to bring the family back together. Children aged 7 and 8 may be more passive than younger children.

Children aged 9-12
Often show anxieties and insecurities, but there can also be anger at the parent who is believed to have caused the separation.

Adolescents aged 13-18
May have a better understanding of the separation, but will suffer from loss of the essential base from which to grow into adulthood and this can lead to destructive and anti-social behaviour. In turn, this can be associated with educational underachievement.

Source: Buchanan and Ten Brinke (1997); adapted from Richards and Dyson (1982)

Children's adjustment to divorce

While children of divorced parents, as a group, have more adjustment problems than do children of never-divorced parents, the view that divorce per se is the major cause of these symptoms must be reconsidered ... the past decade has seen a large increase in studies assessing complex variables which profoundly affect child and adolescent adjustment including marital conflict and violence and related parenting behaviours. (Kelly, 2000, p 963)

How separation affects children

- Most children show distress around the break-up (Richards and Dyson, 1982).
- Many children have adjustment problems long before the family break-up (Elliott and Richards, 1991).
- Some problems associated with children post-parental separation are related to factors consequential to the break-up, such as lower standard of living (Weiss, 1984; Buchanan and Ten Brinke, 1997).

- A few children have long-term adjustment problems (Amato and Keith, 1991; Cherlin et al, 1991; Buchanan and Ten Brinke, 1997).
- Overall, recent research supports the view that the long-term outcome of divorce for the majority of children is resiliency rather than dysfunction (Kelly, 2000).

How conflict between parents affects children

- Children are more likely to have long-term problems where there is conflict between the couple (Rogers and Pryor, 1998).
- It is possible that conflict after divorce is worse for children than conflict within marriage (Hetherington and Stanley-Hagen, 1999).
- Children have fewer problems when they move from conflictual, abusive or neglectful families to more harmonious ones (Hetherington and Stanley-Hagen, 1999).
- Conflict is particularly damaging when it is frequent, intense, physical, unresolved and involves the child (Grych and Fincham, 1999).
- Child's appraisal or understanding of break-up and conflict is important (Grych and Fincham, 1999).
- Children who 'feel caught' in parental conflict are more likely to have poor outcomes (Grych and Fincham, 1999).

Information

- Children need information about the implications for them of their parents' separation (Lyon et al, 1999).
- Some children want to be involved in the decisions that are being made about their future (Lyon et al, 1999; Douglas et al, in press).
- Children may need an independent place for consultation (Lyon et al, 1999).

The implications of domestic violence

- Women are at risk of domestic violence after separating (Hester and Radford, 1996).
- Women's account of violence often fails to come to light (Hester and Radford, 1996).
- There is a close relationship between the safety of mothers and the safety and welfare of children (Hester and Radford, 1996).

Children's adjustment following divorce

Research has moved on since Goldstein, Freud and Solnit (1973) published their controversial book *Before the best interests of the child*. Based on psychoanalytic theory, they argued that every child needed an unbroken relationship with their psychological parent. Their belief was that when parents separated a child could only keep one parental relationship going and that giving the other parent the right to visit was not in the child's best interests. Central to their theory was that the custodial parents should have the right to reject visits from the non-custodial parent.

Research from the US in the late 1970s and 1980s (Hetherington et al, 1985) suggesting that children did better when they maintained contact with both parents after separation, and campaigns by fathers' groups, sparked a change in attitudes. Under the 1989 Children Act previously married parents both retained parental responsibility following divorce and in the 1996 Family Law Act (which is now not to be fully implemented) the court had to have:

... particular regard ... to ... the general principle that, in the absence of evidence to the contrary, the welfare of the child will be best served by his having regular contact with those who have parental responsibility for him and with other members of his family; and the maintenance of as good a continuing relationship with his parents as possible. (1996 Family Law Act, Section 11(4c)

More recently such ideas have been further qualified. A review of current research (Kelly, 2000), bringing together a range of studies from around the world, paints a rather more complex picture of the factors that should be considered when considering what may be 'in the child's best interests'.

The key finding from this research review is that it is hard to generalise what is best for children post-parental separation. Hetherington and Stanley-Hagan (1999) sum up this research by showing the diversity of experiences and family processes. They conclude that how families and children cope post-divorce is related to a complex interaction of risk and protective factors.

Post-divorce factors and child adjustment

Such findings emphasize the need for divorce interventions and legal processes that will promote cooperation and reduce ongoing conflict. (Kelly, 2000, p 15)

Much recent research has focused on the quality of parenting and on parent–child relationships:
- *Risk factors:* erratic, hostile or depressed parenting in the custodial residence; a resident parent with a significant psychiatric or personality disorder.
- *Protective factors:* appropriate emotional support, adequate monitoring of child's activities; appropriate discipline; age-appropriate expectations of child (Buchanan and Ten-Brinke, 1997; Hetherington and Stanley-Hagen, 1999).

Contact
- After the break-up there is a buffering effect of contact with the non-resident parent.
- Large-scale studies have found no relationship between frequency of father contact and child adjustment. What is important is the quality of the father–child relationship.
- A meta-analysis of 57 recent studies shows stronger evidence of the benefits of father–child contact than was thought previously (Amato and Gilbreth, 1999).
- The extent to which the involvement of the father benefits children after parental separation, however, appears to be linked to the degree of conflict, the type of paternal involvement and maternal acceptance, as well as the regular payment of child support.
- Visiting schedules that permit both school-week and leisure time involvement with the non-resident parent may better enable 'real parenting'.

Conflict
- Large-scale studies show that, when conflict is low, adolescents in joint custody were better adjusted, but this was not the case in high-conflict post-divorce families.
- Adolescents who are caught in the middle of their parents' disputes after divorce are more poorly adjusted than those whose parents are in conflict but do not use their children to express their disputes.

Source: Based on the review by Kelly (2000) unless otherwise stated.

The legal framework

The 1989 Children Act

The 1989 Children Act created a new legal framework to deal with the type of disputes which are the topic of this research, based on the concerns of the Law Commission (Law Commission, 1988) that the existing law was not only complex and confusing but made the stakes too high (White et al, 1995).

Since research indicated that children do better after parental separation if they are able to maintain a good relationship with both parents, the Commission argued that where parents can cooperate with each other the law should intervene as little as possible. Section 1(5) of the Act – the so-called 'no order principle' – implemented their recommendation that orders should only be made when the court believed it was the most satisfactory way of safeguarding or promoting the child's welfare.

The Commission also argued that, when parents could not cooperate, the law should try to 'lower the stakes' and avoid the impression that the 'loser loses all'. Accordingly they recommended a new range of orders designed to be 'less emotive'. The overall aim of the powers subsequently enacted in Section 8 of the Children Act, was to concentrate minds on the practical issues rather than on the allocation of theoretical rights and duties, thus avoiding the 'symbolism of victory' that had come to be associated with the old orders (King, 1987; White et al, 1995).

Abolition of the old custody orders and their partial replacement with residence orders was intended to reflect far more than a change in terminology. Fundamental to the Act is the new concept of enduring parental responsibility. Although the precise meaning of the term is 'elusive' (Maclean and Eekelaar, 1997) its significance is that it establishes that parental rights and duties are unaffected by separation. Even a sole residence order does not extinguish the parental responsibility of the non-resident parent (note: currently married parents automatically share parental responsibility; non-married fathers have to acquire parental responsibility either by agreement with the mother or through a court order). The intention is to emphasise the duty on both parents to continue to play a full part in the child's upbringing (DoH, 1989).

The Act was also innovative in recognising the damage that can be done to children by prolonged disputes, requiring that "regard is to be had to the general principle that delay in deciding any question with respect to the child's upbringing is likely to prejudice the child's welfare" (Section 1(2)). Courts were given new powers and duties to manage the progress of the case throughout, rather than leaving it to the parties, although to date this approach would appear to have been only partially effective (Hale, 1995; Hunt, forthcoming).

That the child's welfare is paramount has long been a cardinal principle in children's law. What was new in the Children Act was the attempt to give some structure to what has been recognised as a notoriously indeterminate concept (Bainham, 1998b), through use of the welfare checklist (Section 1(3)), which sets out the minimum factors the court must take into account in determining a disputed private law case. However, its efficacy in delivering the objectives of providing "greater consistency and clarity in the law" and "a more systematic approach to decisions concerning children" (Law Commission, 1988, para 3.17) has not been proven (Bainham, 1998b).

Changing views about residence and contact

Contact

The principle of continuity of contact, which is set out in the UN Convention on the Rights of the Child (Article 9(3)) (UN, 1989), has, until relatively recently, been a key element in UK family law. It is implicit in the Children Act's emphasis on continuing parental responsibility (Bainham, 1998b) and stated explicitly in the 1996 Family Law Act, which, although no longer to be implemented in full, can be seen as a reflection of contemporary received wisdom. It has been held that a presumption of contact had also developed in case law (Bailey-Harris et al, 1998), the general approach being that contact is the right of the child (M v M (child access) [1973] 2 All ER 81), is almost always in the interests of the child (Re O (contact: imposition of conditions) [1995] 2 FLR 124), and that the correct test is whether there are any cogent reasons why contact should be denied (Re H (minors) (access) [1992] 1 FLR 148, [1992] Fam Law 152). A parent who persistently refused contact risked being labelled 'implacably hostile', and even, although rarely, committed to prison for breach of a court order (Re J (a minor) (contact) [1994] 1 FLR 729) and (A v N (committal: refusal of contact) [1997] 1 FLR 533 [1997] Fam Law 233 [1997] 2 FCR 475).

Latterly, however, this approach has been increasingly challenged (Smart and Neale, 1997), particularly in the context of domestic violence (Hester and Radford, 1996; Barnett, 1998; Kaganas, 1999; Radford et al, 1999), with pressure to amend the law to take specific account of domestic violence, as some other countries have done (Advisory Board on Family Law, 1999). Although following a consultation paper on the subject (Advisory Board on Family Law, 1999) it was concluded that this was not necessary, it was also acknowledged that the courts had not been addressing the issue effectively. Guidelines were thus recommended for the judiciary and the Family Court Welfare Service (FCWS) (Advisory Board on Family Law, 2000). By this point the Court of Appeal, which had access to the draft report, had handed down judgments in four key cases involving domestic violence, refusing direct contact in each and putting into effect the principles proposed by the report (Re L (a child) (contact: domestic violence) [2000] 2 FCR 404 [2000] 4 All ER 609 [2000] 2 FLR 334; and other appeals).

Residence

For most of the last century sole custody was the dominant paradigm in family law, the rights of the father as natural guardian (Maclean and Eekelaar, 1997) giving way first to the 'tender years' presumption and then to the concept of the 'psychological parent' (Kurki-Suonio, 2000). This is now being eroded in some jurisdictions by arrangements for shared care and control. The Children Act concept of parental responsibility is a partial expression of this change of approach in relation to the issue of control, and case law has confirmed that pre-Act decisions frowning on shared care are no longer valid (White et al, 1995). While the courts have not yet embraced shared residence as the 'ideal form of custody' (Kurki-Suonio, 2000), as some pressure groups would wish, the approach

appears to be becoming slowly less restrictive (for example, A v A (minors) (shared residence orders) [1995] 1 FCR 91 [1994] 1 FLR 669; Re D (children) (shared residence orders) [2001] Fam Law 183 [2001] 1 FCR 147 [2000] 1 FLR 495).

The position of the child in proceedings

In most public law proceedings under the Children Act children are automatically parties and entitled to representation, usually provided by a solicitor instructed by a guardian ad litem. Although there are some concerns about how this model operates in practice (Murch et al, 1990; Sawyer, 1995; Masson and Winn-Oakley, 1999), these provisions are widely respected as a serious attempt to ensure, not only that the interests of children are promoted, but that their views are taken into account (Cretney, 1990; DoH et al, 1998; Salgo, 1998).

In contrast, in contested private law proceedings under the same Act, although it is possible in exceptional circumstances for the child to be made a party, this is rare. Typically the parties to any action are disputing adults, and the child's interests are deemed to be adequately protected by the court, with the assistance, where necessary, of a report from a FCWO. Such reports, however, are not mandatory (James and Richards, 1999). The position of the FCWO in proceedings is also weaker and less central than that of the guardian ad litem, and there is no lawyer to press the child's case either in negotiations between the parties or in court (Hunt and Lawson, 1999). Finally, although national standards for the FCWS do require officers to see children and give them an opportunity to express their wishes and feelings (Home Office, 1994), there has been concern as to the extent to which they actually do (HM Inspectorate of Probation, 1997; Sawyer, 1999).

This relative disadvantaging of children in private law proceedings has produced considerable pressure for change. Advocates for reform, unsuccessful in their parliamentary lobbying in relation to the Children Bill, did manage to secure an amendment (Section 64) during the passage of the 1996 Family Law Act, which empowered the Lord Chancellor to provide for separate representation of children in certain types of proceedings. However, there was never any certainty that this section would be acted on and now, of course, the Act itself is not to be implemented in full.

However, the creation of the new Children and Family Court Advisory and Support Service (CAFCASS), which brings together practitioners in both private and public law, is likely to increase the already strong pressures to rationalise provision across the two jurisdictions. Respondents to a specific question about representation in the consultation paper that led to the creation of CAFCASS (DoH et al, 1998) in the main took the view that, while separate representation was not needed for all children in private law disputes, it should be more widely available. Article 12 of the UN Convention on the Rights of the Child provides another impetus to change, as does Article 6 of the European Convention on Human Rights. Indeed, in a recent case, the President of the Family Division has stated:

I suspect that as a result of the Human Rights convention becoming part of domestic law and the increased view of the English courts, in any event, that the children should be seen and heard in child cases and are not always sufficiently seen and heard by the use of a court welfare officer's report, there will be an increased use of guardians in private law cases. Indeed, in the right case, I would welcome it. (A v A (contact: representation of child's interests) 20 November 2000)

The questions then become: What is the right case? How and by whom is the issue to be decided? Should there be specific criteria, and if so what should they be? Or should the issue be decided on a case-by-case basis, which allows for considerable flexibility but risks wide and arbitrary variation?

Decision making within family proceedings

The process

All parents who separate need to make decisions about the arrangements for their children, in particular who they will live with and how they maintain a relationship with the other parent. Some parents will make these decisions on their own, some with the help of solicitors, some following mediation and some by going to court. What was appropriate

for a child at one stage of their life may need to be changed as they get older. Parents and children will take these decisions in different ways at different stages in a child's life.

Figure 1.2 illustrates, in broad terms, the decision-making process and options for parents in the years after their separation.

Family Court Welfare Services

If a parent decides that they cannot reach an agreement with their former partner, either informally or through mediation or solicitors, they have the option of applying to a family court for an order.

> **Orders available under Section 8 of the 1989 Children Act**
> - Residence
> - Contact
> - Specific issues
> - Prohibited steps

Section 7 of the 1989 Children Act allows a court that has been asked to make a decision about a child to order a welfare report. At the time the research was conducted, welfare reports were prepared by FCWOs, who were employed by the local probation service. Probation committees had been required by the 1967 Matrimonial Causes Act to appoint a FCWO to every divorce county court (DoH et al, 1998). By the time the research was undertaken FCWOs were providing welfare reports to all levels of courts: family proceedings courts (magistrates' courts), county courts and the High Court. In 1997, nearly 700 FCWOs were employed by 53 local probation services.

A welfare report

The purpose of a welfare report is to give the court sufficient information about the circumstances of a child to allow it to take a decision in the child's best interests (Home Office, 1994). In the spirit of promoting parental responsibility, a FCWO may help parents reach an agreement. However, the national standards make it clear that the role of the FCWO is primarily investigative.

Figure 1.2: The welfare reporting process

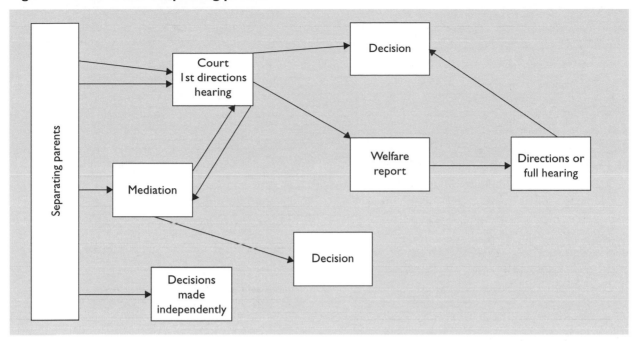

In order to prepare the report FCWOs will interview the parents. National standards require FCWOs to see all children "unless there are strong grounds for not doing so". Other professionals, such as teachers and health visitors who know the children, may also be contacted. Checks will be made with the police for criminal records or to ascertain whether the child is known to the local social services department.

Within these parameters, the way in which a welfare report is prepared can vary markedly between one probation service area and another, and indeed between teams within the same area (James and Hay, 1993). For example, in some areas, children are routinely seen at home whereas in others children are normally seen at the FCWS office. It has been noted earlier in this chapter that the inspection report suggested that many children were not interviewed (HM Inspectorate of Probation, 1997). In some areas, parents are usually invited for an initial interview together and in others the normal practice is for parents to be seen separately. In some teams two officers may be present during interviews, in others this rarely happens. The different approaches reflect different team cultures and individual preferences rather than being based on research evidence.

Under the 1989 Children Act courts are required to consider the 'welfare checklist' when a decision is made about a child. In order to provide useful information to the courts, FCWOs will use the same checklist to assess a child's needs and report on the child's wishes.

The welfare checklist

A court shall have regard to:
- the ascertainable wishes and feelings of the child taking into account the child's age and understanding;
- the child's physical, emotional and educational needs;
- the likely effect on the child of any change in circumstances;
- the child's age, gender, background and relevant characteristics;
- any harm the child has suffered or is at risk of suffering;
- how capable each of the parents, and any other person in relation to whom the court considers the question to be relevant, is of meeting the child's needs;
- the range of powers available to the court under the Act. (1989 Children Act, Section 1(3))

The Children and Family Court Advisory and Support Service (CAFCASS)

Until April 2001, two other services besides the FCWS provided advice to the courts in family proceedings. These were the 59 guardian ad litem panels in England and Wales, who provided guardians ad litem for children who were subject of care or related proceedings, and the Office of the Official Solicitor which, through its 60 staff, represented children at the high and county court level in proceedings of unusual moral or legal complexity (DoH et al, 1998).

In July 1999, after consultation, the government announced that the functions of the three services would be provided by CAFCASS, set up as a non-departmental public body under the Lord Chancellor's Department (LCD). CAFCASS came into being on 1 April 2001.

The function of CAFCASS

In family proceedings where the welfare of children may be in question, CAFCASS must:
- safeguard and promote the welfare of children;
- give advice to any court about any application made to it in the proceedings;
- make provision for children to be represented;
- provide information, advice and other support for the children and their families. (2000 Criminal and Court Services Act, Section 12(1))

In spite of the organisational change, there has been no change in the legal framework. The courts will still ask for welfare reports in proceedings when there is a dispute about children. Initially the same staff will be performing the same functions as they were prior to creation of CAFCASS, although, as noted earlier, under CAFCASS the FCWOs became Children and Family Reporters. From April 2001, change in practice will be evolutionary.

This research

Under the UN *Convention on the rights of the child* (1989, Clauses 12-17) and the 1989 Children Act, children and young people of sufficient age and understanding have a right to be involved in decisions affecting their lives. In a democratic society, every citizen also has a right to a fair and just legal process. In 1999 there were 36,142 welfare reports were prepared, involving more than 60,000 children. The FCWS alone cost in 1999 around £35 million per annum. Despite its significance for a great many children and their parents, for judicial decision making and for limited public sector resources, welfare reporting is a very underresearched area.

This research provided a means of enabling parents and children involved in a court welfare report to voice their opinion and give an independent evaluation of the degree to which these rights were respected in the family justice system. The research is also of particular interest because it is the first to explore outcomes, following up parents and children a year after proceedings had ended.

Summary

- This research is taking place against a background of change: changing families, changing attitudes to family life, new knowledge about the consequences of separation and divorce on children and now the creation of a new agency, CAFCASS – part of whose responsibility will be to respond to the needs of children whose separated parents cannot agree about the arrangements for their children.
- The FCWS cost in 1999 around £35 million per annum and involved more than 60,000 children. Despite the significance of welfare reporting for a great many children and parents, for judicial decision making and for limited public sector resources, very little is known about what happens after the court proceedings.
- It is hoped that, as the first study to explore outcomes, this report will inform the new agency and help bring about an improvement in the way decisions are made about children.

Note

[1] Throughout this study reference is made to FCWOs, the title of these staff when the research was undertaken. There was a change of title but not of role or personnel when the Children and Family Court Advisory and Support Service (CAFCASS) was established on 1 April 2001 and FCWOs became Children and Family Reporters.

2

Portrait of the families and their disputes

The Act rests on the belief that children are generally best looked after within the family with both parents playing a full part and without resort to legal proceedings. (DoH, 1989, p 1)

Following separation many children lose contact with the parent they are not living with. As Maclean and Eekelaar (1997) have shown, even among previously married couples where levels of post-separation contact were highest, contact was only occurring in around two thirds of cases, dropping to one half when couples had cohabited and a third when the parents had never lived together. The parents in this study were therefore somewhat unusual in that central to most of their disputes was the desire of the non-resident parent to play a greater part in their children's lives. They were also unusual in that they had been unable to resolve their disputes without recourse to the courts. Many had been to court on previous occasions.

Parents' litigation history

Just under half the sample (48%) consisted of cases coming to court for the first time. The remainder reflected a wide range of experience, from cases returning to court for review to those in which there had been several sets of proceedings over a number of years. In order to accommodate the disparity in parental experience and assess whether this made any difference to the perspectives of those interviewed, a typology of cases was constructed (see opposite and Figure 2.1).

The parents
- 100 parents, 73 cases.
- 52% mothers, 48% fathers.
- 37% cases both parents interviewed.
- Previously married couples: 55%; cohabited: 34%; other: 11%.
- Age range 19 to 58 years; median 37 years.
- Average duration of relationship pre-separation 6 years; range 6 months to 20 years.
- Diversity of occupational groups: manual, skilled, professional, managerial, owners of small businesses and company directors.
- Wide range of household income but almost one third on income support.
- In 60% of cases one or both parents known to be legally aided.
- Both parents white, 60% cases; same ethnic minority group, 22% cases; different ethnic origin, 18% cases (see Appendix B for a full breakdown of ethnic identities).

Ligitant type
- *First-timers:* first set of proceedings; a welfare report was not part of a review.
- *Returners:* proceedings were a planned review of previous decision.
- *Revivers:* there had been previous proceedings but these finished more than two years ago.
- *Repeaters:* those returning to court within a two-year period.
- *Perpetual litigants:* the number of proceedings exceeds the years since separation or there have been continuous proceedings over a number of years.

Figure 2.1: Litigant typology

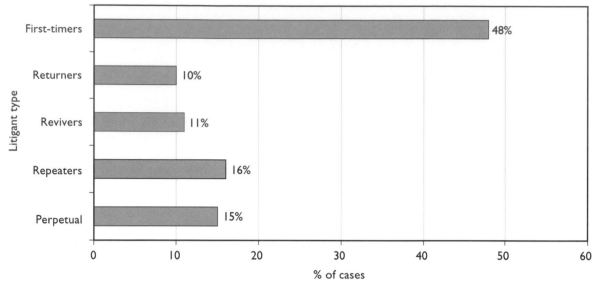

Note: *n*=73.

The current dispute

For the most part parents were arguing about contact, with more than eight out of ten cases involving an application for a contact order compared to only a third for residence. These figures reflect the national picture in which contact applications far outweigh residence (LCD, 2000a).

As others have pointed out (Bailey-Harris et al, 1998), some residence applications may essentially be about contact and there were a few of these 'tactical' applications in our sample. Conversely, some applications for contact were really about residence. These were typically cases in which non-resident fathers were already enjoying regular staying contact, wanted to play a full part in their children's day-to-day lives but did not feel able to apply for shared residence. As the example opposite illustrates, these disputes were among the most bitter in the sample, even though on paper the parents were only arguing about the details of contact, not the principle.

In Figures 2.2 and 2.3, percentages are given for those cases in which the *main* issue was residence or the *main* issue was contact.

In all types of dispute the vast majority of applicants were non-resident fathers (78%), ranging from 92% in contact disputes to 50% in cases where residence was the main issue. Although only a minority of disputes were about the principle of contact (Figure 2.3), at the point proceedings started contact had been suspended in two out of three cases. In general, however, this represented a break in the normal pattern, there being only 12 cases in which contact had not been taking place at all. Suspending contact was therefore being used as a strategy to deal with a whole range of difficulties between parents and was not necessarily regarded by the resident parent as more than a transitory state of affairs.

Indeed, it was clear that in some instances mothers had deliberately broken off contact as a way of either forcing their ex-partner to change his behaviour or to provoke him into taking the case to court. One mother, for instance, stopped contact because of suspicions that the father, who had been having weekly staying contact for two years, was once again abusing drugs. She explained that:

> "I wanted him to come off drugs and for them to spend quality time with him. I would never want to stop contact permanently, I wouldn't do that to the children; they love him to bits."

Example

The children have lived with mother since their parents separated three years ago, and this was the fifth set of proceedings. The application was for variation to staying contact; residence has never been contested. The quote is taken from the first interview with father.

"I realise now that I should have issued proceedings straightaway. That's the only way the children would have got what they wanted out of it – equal time with both their parents. But I was working 50 miles away at the time so I thought at the moment it's got to be like this but I'd put my feelers out for a job [nearby].

"She then moved. I went to see my solicitor and said, 'Look this isn't bloody on, I've had my children taken away and get dictated to all the time', but he was very much, 'Let's take the conflict out of it, it's not the time to kick up a fuss, give her time, give her space', all that nonsense. I said, 'Let's take her to court and fight this out'. But he said, 'You won't get anywhere, there's no point'. I was left with, 'I can see them every other weekend and some of the holidays'. Bearing in mind that before the separation I was looking after the children for a minimum of four nights a week from the moment I got in from work until they went to bed because my ex-wife worked. So I was a major player in a formative time.

"When we went to court [the first time] I tried to make the point that she had just cleared off but everyone was of the opinion that was in the past and immaterial and a new status quo had been established..."

Researcher: "Were you applying for shared residence then?"

"I was told not to bother, that I should think myself lucky I had that much contact. The barrister said, 'Most of my punters don't get that. I would put up with it; you're very, very lucky'.

"I've never got what I wanted and I've never got what I think is in the best interests of the children. It takes two people to make a child and children want to spend half their time with mummy and half with daddy. And the time is fast approaching when that will become reality because there are a lot of fathers in this country who accept that mothers play a role as well but that the child doesn't need one parent or the other, the child needs both."

Dispute resolution prior to proceedings

Government policy has increasingly sought to divert parents from the litigation process, with all its attendant financial and emotional costs. It would appear that many of the parents in this sample subscribed to this perspective in that, in over two thirds of the cases, parents reported trying to resolve the current dispute in other ways before resorting to the court. Half had tried to sort it out for themselves, sometimes with help from their wider family. Just under half had involved one or more outside agencies, such as counselling or mediation services, solicitors, or social workers. There were 12 cases in which counselling or mediation had been considered but rejected, almost always because of the refusal of one party to participate. In a further 10 cases counselling/mediation had been tried but both parents had rarely stayed the course.

Those coming to the court for the first time were more likely to have tried parental or family negotiation but less likely to have involved outside agencies. This may mean that parents who had already been through the process were more aware of the wider range of services available and more willing to try them, or perhaps less optimistic about what recourse to law could achieve.

Despite the increase in children's litigation since the Children Act, the parents interviewed in this project displayed none of the "apparent enthusiasm for litigation" suggested by Davis (Davis, 2000, p 136). Indeed, the weariness with which most of the parents spoke about their encounters with the law suggests rather that most are litigating with every appearance of despair and frustration. Moreover, when parents who were interviewed in the second stage of the research were asked whether they thought mediation should be compulsory before court proceedings started 60% agreed and 15% 'sort of agreed'; only a quarter disagreed.

Figure 2.2: Residence the main issue

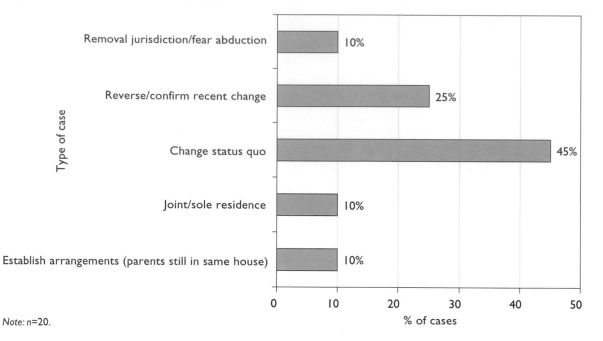

Note: n=20.

Figure 2.3: Contact the main issue: the dispute

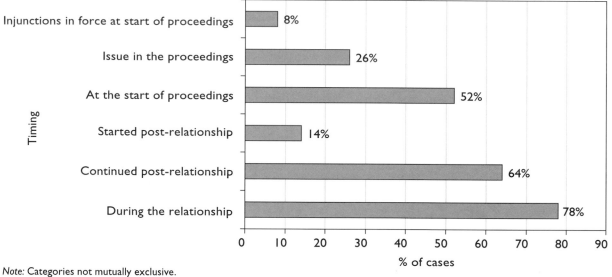

Note: Categories not mutually exclusive.
n=53 cases.

The parental relationship

As might be expected, the majority of parents at the point proceedings were instigated described relationships that were at best very poor and at worst highly conflicted. They summed these up in words such as "poisonous", "nasty", "vitriolic", "horrendous" and "stormy". There were only two cases in which relationships were said to be 'not that bad', while in 24% there was said to be no relationship at all. Face-to-face communication was taking place between only a quarter of couples, although a further 16% were able to speak to each other over the telephone. In 29% of cases, there was said to be no communication at all, while the rest were communicating only through family intermediaries or outside agencies, usually solicitors.

> "It was an armed truce at all times, but this was a low point."
>
> "We have been rowing for two-and-a-half years – ever since the divorce."
>
> "It's always been nasty; a terrible time. We've been to court over everything. It's been an ongoing battle."

As these quotes illustrate, most parents also described a relationship that had been poor since the point of separation or had become even worse over time. There were only a handful in which either there was said to have been some improvement or the relationship had never been particularly conflict-ridden or difficult.

Domestic violence

We know that one woman in four experiences domestic violence at some stage in her life and it is estimated that between one in eight and one in ten has experienced domestic violence in the past year. (Cabinet Office and Home Office, 1999)

Given the concerns that have been voiced about the response of the family justice system to domestic violence, domestic violence was clearly a key topic for the research to explore. A broad definition of what constituted violence was adopted and where an interviewee had not already broached the subject themselves (which very many of them had) they were asked: 'Was there ever a point in your relationship with your ex-partner, either before or after you split up, when you were frightened of him/her or s/he might have felt frightened of you?'. This needs to be borne in mind in considering the findings, not to minimise the problem, but to be clear that, unless otherwise specified, we are not speaking only of physical violence. This is particularly important in relation to post-separation experiences where we found that, although there was often still very real fear about an ex-partner, assaults were rare.

Nonetheless, it was surprising, even in this high conflict group, to find such a high incidence of violent, abusive and intimidating relationships, with at least one parent reporting fear at some point in more than three in four cases (78%) and over half (56%)

reporting physical violence (see Figure 2.4). Across the three areas – rural, urban and inner-city – the percentage of parents reporting domestic violence was very similar. It is likely that these figures are an underestimate, given that men are believed to underreport violence to themselves and that, when couples were interviewed, there was rarely agreement about whether violence had occurred. Women were rarely describing occasional or minor incidents – two thirds reporting violence as a frequent or almost constant feature of their relationship, and injuries ranging from severe bruising to broken bones and internal injuries as well as sustained harassment, emotional abuse and intimidation.

The proportion of mother interviewees reporting violence (or, more commonly, fear) to be continuing at the point proceedings started reduced to one half (Figure 2.5). Moreover, only just over a quarter regarded domestic violence as an issue in the proceedings. This apparent withering away of the issue was a source of disquiet in the course of the research, for, while there was confidence that the interviewees had been given every opportunity to recount their experiences, it was possible that the sample missed the most severe cases. This was the primary reason for undertaking analysis of a larger sample through scrutiny of the welfare reports (see Appendix A for further details). Although it was recognised that this process could not possibly uncover the 'true' incidence of violence, it was judged it should indicate whether cases in which domestic violence was recognised to be a major issue in proceedings were missing. However, this process showed almost identical proportions in each sample.

Child welfare and safety concerns

It is estimated that about three children per 1,000 were on child protection registers at 31 March 1998. It is further estimated that around 3% of children at any one moment are 'children in need' (DoH, 2001). In this study only 116 children were involved so, given a normal population, it would have been unlikely that any children would have been on the child protection register and only three or so would have been known to social services as children in need.

Figure 2.4: Type of violence

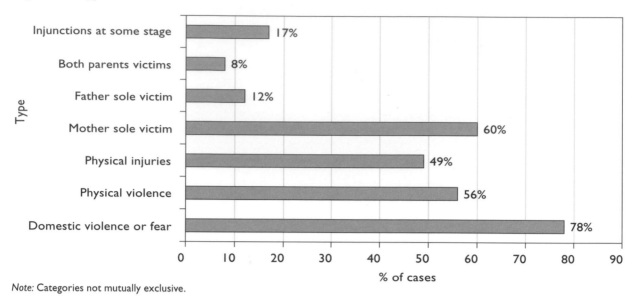

Note: Categories not mutually exclusive.

Figure 2.5: The timing of domestic violence

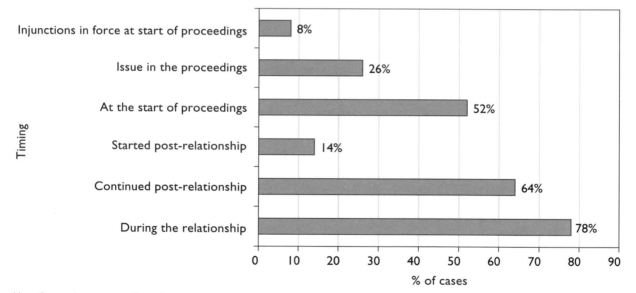

Note: Categories not mutually exclusive.

From the parents' accounts (see Figure 2.6), it was apparent that there were *current* social service concerns in 4% of cases, while more than a third of the cases had at some time been linked with social services. There were alcohol problems involved in more than one in five cases and drug abuse in one in ten; in more than a quarter of cases possible mental illness was mentioned. It was interesting that these child protection concerns were generally underreported in the welfare report but, even so, in a third of the cases, child safety issues were mentioned in the report.

These figures may underrepresent the true extent of child protection concerns in such cases. When the welfare reports of those who took part in this research were compared with a random sample of all cases coming to the family court services in the three areas, it was found that the study sample underrepresented cases involving more serious child protection issues (see Appendix A for methodology).

Figure 2.6: Cases in which there were concerns about child welfare

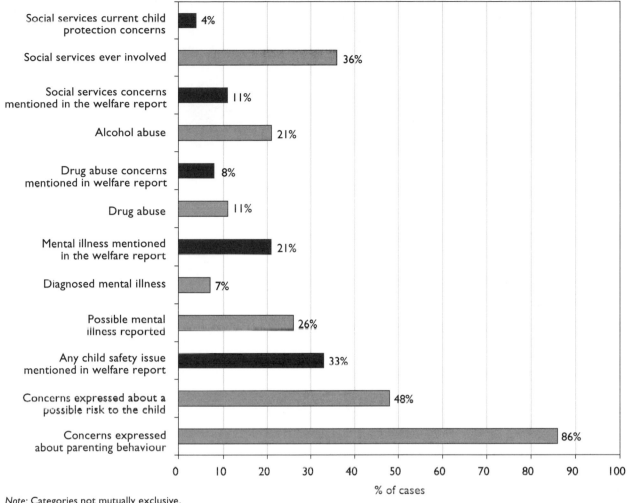

Social services current child protection concerns — 4%
Social services ever involved — 36%
Social services concerns mentioned in the welfare report — 11%
Alcohol abuse — 21%
Drug abuse concerns mentioned in welfare report — 8%
Drug abuse — 11%
Mental illness mentioned in the welfare report — 21%
Diagnosed mental illness — 7%
Possible mental illness reported — 26%
Any child safety issue mentioned in welfare report — 33%
Concerns expressed about a possible risk to the child — 48%
Concerns expressed about parenting behaviour — 86%

% of cases

Note: Categories not mutually exclusive.
n=73.

Apart from these more serious concerns, one of the striking features of the interviews was the frequency with which parents reported worries about the parenting behaviour or capacity of their ex-partner. Mothers and fathers were equally likely to express concerns and there were no differences by ethnic background. As might be expected, however, mothers for whom domestic violence was a key issue in the proceedings were the most likely to be anxious.

While some of these concerns did not amount to fears for the safety of the children, they nevertheless weighed heavily as a reason for opposing the other parent's proposals. Many parents were worried by the different approach to parenting adopted by their ex-partner, either because they did not support such an approach or they believed it was difficult for the child

to adapt to different expectations and family cultures. One parent might smack, for example, while the other never used physical punishment. There might be different household routines or no discernible routine. Some fathers had little experience of caring for a small child on their own and the mothers were not confident that they could cope.

"He doesn't think about the children's needs. He forgets to feed them. They have no meal times and he just does his own thing." (Mother)

"I didn't know where they were sleeping when they were with the mother. There were seven children altogether in the house and two lodgers. I didn't want to question the children but I didn't like the instability and lack of routine." (Father)

Other anxieties related to more risky situations: past physical abuse, for example, substance abuse, driving while drunk, inadequate supervision and neglect.

The priority to be given to a child's social activities was another, often bitter, source of conflict between parents. Some children would have needed a nine-day week to fit their extracurricular activities in with the level of contact expected by the non-resident parent, as well as spending time with their resident parent. As children got older, more parents described the difficulty the children had in negotiating their commitments.

The children: experiences and well-being

The children
- 116 children subject to proceedings.
- All except four were children of both parties.
- 52% boys, 48% girls.
- Ages: up to seven 56%; eight to eleven 34%; twelve to sixteen 10%.
- Residence: living with mother 86%; with father 10%; shared care 4%.
- Ethnicity: white 60%; Asian 14%; African/African Caribbean 10%; mixed heritage 16%.

Given what is now known about the impact of parental conflict and domestic violence on children (see Chapter 1), the picture presented by the parents of their relationships pre- and post-separation is ominous. In over two thirds of cases children were said to have witnessed arguments; half of them either 'quite often' or 'very often'. Just under a third were said to have witnessed violence, with a few more being aware of it. We also have information directly from the 30 children interviewed in stage two and, in response to pre-set questions, two thirds said they were aware of their parents arguing and more than a third that their parents had 'pushed' or 'shoved' each other.

As will be seen in Chapter 8, standardised measures of well-being completed by parents at the end of proceedings and 12 months later showed that all the children, not just those interviewed, scored much higher on levels of emotional distress scales than children in the general population, with those who had witnessed domestic violence coming out as the most distressed of all.

Summary

- The sample parents were highly diverse in terms of their ethnic background (40% of cases were from ethnic minority groups or mixed parentage), their income level (some families had very high incomes but almost one third were on income support; in more than 60% one or both parents was legally aided), the nature and duration of their relationship (average duration was six years but ranged from six months to twenty years), and their experience of family law proceedings (43% of cases had previously been to court).
- The disputes in under a third of cases were about residence and the rest concerned contact arrangements.
- Physical violence, or the fear of violence, had been an issue for at least one parent in four out of five cases.
- 86% of the children were living with their mother at the start of the proceedings, 10% with their father and 4% were in a shared-care arrangement.

3

The court proceedings

Section 1 of the Children Act 1989 sets out three principles which guide a court making decisions under the Act.

The first is that the child's welfare is the paramount consideration when a court determines any questions with respect to his upbringing ('the welfare principle').

The second is that the court should not make an order under the Act unless it considers that to do so would be better for the children than making no order at all.

The third is that the court should have regard to the general principle that delay in determining a question with respect to the upbringing of children is likely to prejudice his welfare. (DoH, 1989, p 16)

Parental perspectives on outcome

Orders and outcomes

As noted above, proceedings under the Children Act are governed by the so-called 'no order' principle. However, in these highly conflicted cases, more than eight out of ten ended with an order being made. Moreover, of the remaining completed cases all but one ended with either the applicant father withdrawing or having the case dismissed in his absence. The only true 'no order' case was one in which the parents agreed joint care and all existing orders were rescinded.

Table 3.1: Outcomes of disputes where residence was the main issue (%)

Cases ending in residence order	80
Orders in favour of applicant	
Mother (*n*=7)	57
Father (*n*–13)	15
Non resident father (*n*−10)	10
Non-resident mother (*n*=4)	50
Residence (*n*=20)	
Remained with mother	50
Remained with father	15
Remained shared	5
Changed in favour of father	15
Changed in favour of mother	15

Note: n=20.

The frustration of the sample fathers (and fathers generally who would like to apply for residence orders) can be understood against the background of the data, which show overwhelmingly that children live with their mothers and court applications do not often change this pattern (Table 3.1). It was notable, for instance, that only one of the ten applications by a non-resident father in which residence was the main issue was successful, compared to two of the four by non-resident mothers. Moreover, in some cases, it seemed likely that the outcome would have been different had positions been reversed. In one case, for example, the mother had had serious alcohol problems, resulting in her child being placed on the child protection register; the father was given a residence order. By the time proceedings started the mother's health had improved and a joint residence order was made, despite the father's opposition. Would the court have made such an order to a non-resident father in this position?

Given what has been argued to be a presumption of contact in private law (Bailey-Harris et al, 1998), the proportion of contact disputes ending in no direct contact is surprisingly high, particularly where contact was being opposed either in principle or because of the child's opposition (Table 3.2). These cases also account for a disproportionate number of unsuccessful applications by non-resident fathers. In all other types of contact dispute fathers stood at least a 50:50, and usually much better, chance of success.

Table 3.2: Outcomes where contact was the main dispute (%)

Cases ending in contact order (*n*=39)	74
Order in favour of applicant, by dispute*	
Principle of contact opposed (*n*=10)	25
Child resistant (*n*=8)	13
Contact not opposed but problematic (*n*=5)	80
Supervised/unsupervised (*n*=7)	33
Staying/visiting (*n*=3)	33
Details of contact (*n*=20)	50
Orders in favour of	
Applicant mother (*n*=4)	25
Applicant father (*n*=13)	49
Outcome (*n*=39)*	
No contact	18
Indirect only	18
Supervised	13
Visiting, unsupervised	18
Staying	54

Note: * categories not mutually exclusive.
n=53.

Satisfaction with outcome

Although overall only 40 of the 100 parents interviewed were entirely positive about the outcome of proceedings, only a small minority (22) were completely negative. Even among the unsuccessful applicants interviewed only a third (8 of 24) were entirely dismissive. There were no statistical differences by gender, applicant or residence status although as Figure 3.1 shows, some differences were apparent.

It was notable that although only a third of all applicants (14 of the 41 answering the question) thought that they had achieved *everything* they wanted in bringing proceedings, less than a quarter (10) said they had achieved *nothing*. Although the proportion was inevitably higher among unsuccessful applicants, it did not exceed one third either in contact or in residence disputes. Proceedings therefore are at least delivering some, if not all the goods, at least as far as applicants are concerned.

Responses in the 27 cases (Figure 3.2) in which both parents were interviewed were also unexpected, in that only five 'couples' held diametrically opposed views on outcome, while the largest group consisted of parents expressing the same level of satisfaction.

Figure 3.1: Satisfaction with court outcome (%)

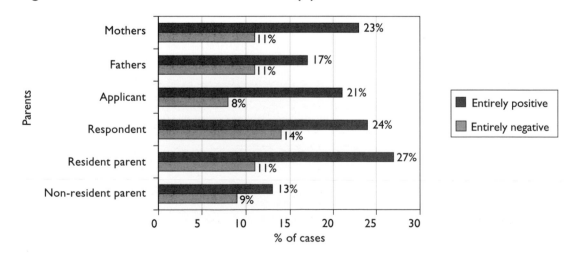

Figure 3.2: Comparison of parental satisfaction in cases where both parents were interviewed (%)

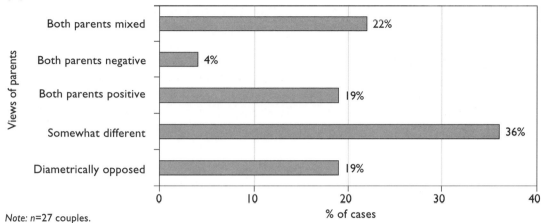

Note: n=27 couples.

Figure 3.3: Satisfaction with the court outcome (%)

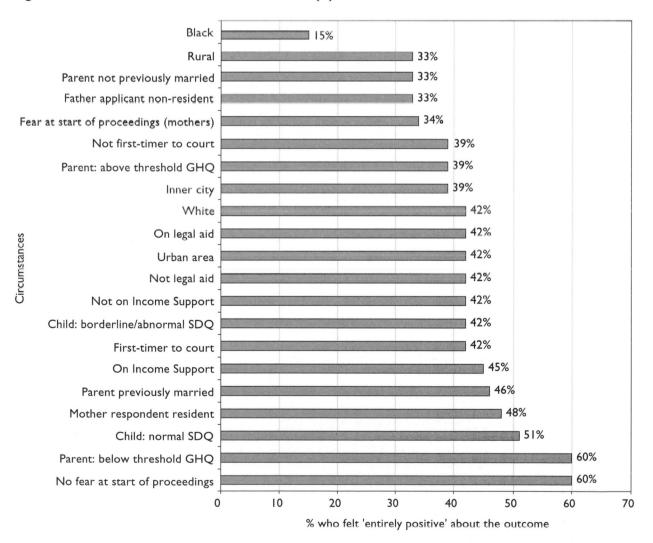

Note: GHQ = General Health Questionnaire; SDQ = Strengths and Difficulties Questionnaire.

Differing levels of satisfaction with the court outcome by parental and child circumstances

It was apparent that categorising parents into groups of mothers or fathers, applicants or respondents, resident or non-resident, did not indicate how different parents in very different circumstances fared. In a small study numbers are rarely large enough to reach levels of statistical significance, nevertheless it was felt important to give some indication of who felt they came out best following the court proceedings.

Figure 3.3 gives percentages of those in each category who were 'entirely positive' about the court outcome. For example the first bar shows the percentage of black parents who were 'entirely positive' about the outcome. Towards the bottom of the figure the percentage is given for white parents. It is apparent that black parents were less positive about the court outcome than white.

At the fourth bar, we see that only 33% of applicant non-resident fathers were 'entirely positive' whereas, to the bottom of the figure, we see 48% of resident mothers were 'entirely positive', suggesting, as the previous discussion would support, that fathers felt less positive about the court outcome.

Similarly, 34% of mothers who expressed fear of possible violence at the start of the proceedings felt positive about the outcome, compared with 60% of those mothers who did not such express fear. The figure also refers to parents who had a General Health Questionnaire (GHQ) score above threshold, which is a measure of significant emotional dysfunction, while those with a score below threshold would be those parents who were apparently coping quite well with the situation. Children's emotional well-being was measured by whether their Strengths and Difficulties Questionnaire (SDQ) score was within the 'normal' range or within the 'borderline or abnormal' range indicating significant adjustment problems. The figure suggests that parents whose children were not exhibiting significant emotional and behavioural problems (that is, their children were within the normal SDQ range) were also fairly satisfied with the court outcome. Further details of parents and children's well-being are given in Chapter 8. (Full

details of the categories used in Figure 3.3 are given in Appendix A.)

The differences between many of the categories, if they exist at all, are small, but Figure 3.3 indicates that, at the extremes, some groups of parents were considerably more satisfied than others.

Perspectives on the process of dispute resolution

According to Davis (1997), private law proceedings are so imbued with a settlement-seeking ethos that "to get to the point of adjudication one needs the resolve and momentum of a battleship". It is perhaps a measure of the degree of conflict in the sample cases that a third of cases went to a fully or partially contested hearing, with just under a third of cases settling at the door of the court and just over a third settling before the day of hearing.

As might be expected there was a relationship between the point at which settlement was reached and parental views on outcome with two thirds of parents whose cases were settled prior to the day of the hearing expressing wholly positive views compared to a third of those settling at the door of the court or going to a contested hearing.

Dispute resolution prior to the day of the final hearing

One in five parents reported that at least some issues had been settled *before the welfare report was filed*. However, only four cases were resolved completely in this period. Nor did resolution necessarily mean that it was the process of preparing the welfare report that made the difference. One couple, for example, reached agreement before they even saw the welfare officer. One father dropped his application because his daughter told him she wanted the contact arrangements to stay as they were. But there were at least four out of 73 cases in which the FCWO did appear to be influential. As one father put it:

"She did bring us together and made us both think very carefully about what was going on and whether any change in position was possible."

Another father felt he had no option but to abandon his application for residence in view of what he perceived to be the FCWO's dismissive attitude.

In general, those who voiced an opinion on dispute resolution were fairly positive about the extent to which their disagreements had been resolved, with a third expressing entirely positive or mixed views and only one in ten being entirely negative. Among those who were entirely positive, two groups could be discerned: those who had 'won' because their ex-partner had backed down and those who described what appeared to be a genuine agreement resulting from both parents shifting position.

In contrast, all those who held entirely negative views seemed to feel that they had given in:

> "I thought that [ex-partner] would get their own way, and going to court would be pointless and too much hassle."

Of the cases in which at least some elements of the dispute had been resolved during the welfare enquiry only five went to a full hearing. Three of these actually settled at the door of the court, suggesting that movement towards agreement during the course of the welfare enquiry may promote settlement.

On the whole, parents whose cases did settle before the day of the final hearing were fairly positive about the process. More than half expressed a wholly positive opinion, while a quarter was ambivalent and only a small proportion was wholly negative. There was no difference between men and women. Of the six 'couple' cases, however, while all the mothers were entirely positive only three of the fathers were.

Relief that they would not have to face the uncertainty and stress of the court hearing was a key theme in the responses:

> "I was very relieved that he [the father] had changed his mind. I actually thanked him for doing that. I had been dreading a court hearing, it sounded such a big affair." (Mother)

> "You take your chance when you go into court. I hoped it would be the best way forward." (Mother)

Given the predominantly positive views expressed by these parents it is perhaps not unexpected that few of them reported feeling subject to pressure to reach agreement, although this was a question explicitly put to them. However, it is of note that six of the seven parents who did report feeling under pressure were mothers.

> "It was out of my hands; the solicitor said, 'You've got to give him something'." (Mother who said she felt she had no alternative but to agree to contact)

> "The solicitor said he stood a 99% chance of getting what he wanted if it went to court." (Mother who agreed to more staying contact than she wanted and, it transpired, more than the FCWO was going to recommend)

Pressure was usually identified as coming from one or more persons involved in the case (the solicitor, the FCWO, the other partner). One mother, however, said that it was considerations of cost that had put her under pressure to agree, while a father simply said that he realised he had no other options: "my back was against the wall".

There was a close relationship between satisfaction with the dispute resolution process and views about outcome. Nevertheless, there were some exceptions, including six parents who were entirely satisfied with the outcome but voiced some negative opinions about the process, and five who held mixed views about the outcome but were entirely satisfied or entirely dissatisfied with the process.

Settlement at the door of the court

In contrast to parents who resolved their disputes before the final hearing who mainly voiced firm and positive views about the process, ambivalence was the dominant opinion for nearly half of the parents who settled at the door of the court. Moreover, among those who held a firm opinion, more were negative than positive. Across the whole group, pressure to settle, reported by a much higher proportion of parents resolving their dispute at the door of the court, also appears to have been exerted more or less evenly on men and women.

In the eight 'couple' cases there were six in which parents' opinions differed. In three the mother was more negative, in three the father. Mothers in these couple cases were slightly more likely to report feeling under pressure to settle than their ex-partners.

Lawyers were again seen as the main source of pressure:

> "[It was a] heated discussion; all guns blazing. The barristers applied collective pressure on me; I was under pressure to agree to conditions. I had to give way." (Father)

> "It was forced upon me – my solicitor said I wouldn't get any concessions out of [mother]." (Father)

However, pressure coming from the judge, an ex-partner or the FCWO was also mentioned. Some parents did not identify a person as the source of pressure, but instead referred to their own wish to avoid the trauma or the cost of a contested hearing.

> "The judge asked if we had reached some form of understanding and we said, 'not really', so he gave us some time. [Father] used that time to go backwards and forwards and make demands.... I was paying my barrister on an hourly rate, and I arrived at 10am and expected to be out at 1pm at the most. It was going on and on and on. I felt I was put in a position where I had to compromise ... because the problem that was in the back of my mind was that I had just spent the whole day in court and spent £475 on a barrister; I have paid £500 for my solicitor. If this doesn't get sorted I will pay another £1,000 on another day. I had to agree to do something for my child that I hadn't even asked her if she wanted to do. I was forced into it...." (Mother)

A few other parents also subsequently regretted the decision they had made under pressure.

> "I compromised more than I wanted; I thought it was better to negotiate than be judged – I don't trust judges; so I compromised on times, there were things not covered in the agreement. I was making the decision on what my solicitor told me, on the welfare report and the fact that I was so stressed I couldn't.... I was coerced into it by lack of finances. It feels unfair; now I am kicking myself." (Mother)

Views on outcome were again the best predictor of satisfaction with the settlement process although there were some exceptions, most notably that, although eleven parents were entirely positive about the outcome, only four were completely positive about the process.

Davis has written extensively about the 'settlement-seeking ethos' which characterises family cases, memorably likening the attitude of the court to that of "a butcher's shop which will not sell meat" (Davis, 1997). The ambivalent response of the parents in this group and the high proportion that reported feeling under pressure to settle was therefore not unexpected. What was surprising, however, was the response in the second stage of the research to specific questions about settlement seeking. More than three quarters of respondents said that parents should be strongly encouraged to reach agreement, but less than half considered that they had been or that courts did everything they could to encourage agreement, and only a third thought that parents were put under pressure. Indeed, on the basis of this research, it would seem that not only is the butcher reluctant to sell, the customers are not that certain that they want to buy. One reason for this is likely to be parents' experiences of contested court hearings.

Dispute only completely settled through court hearing

Just under a third of cases went to a partially or fully contested hearing. Four out of five of the responses recorded were entirely negative about the experience. Also, strikingly, of the 'couples' responding to the question half were agreed in how negative the experience had been – perhaps the only thing they did agree on.

Negative comments generally fell into two groups. Some parents perceived the hearing to be a foregone conclusion, describing it as "irrelevant", "a farce" and "a waste of time". Most, however, referred to the trauma of the occasion, which was "horrible" and "intimidating", even, for one father, "the single most stressful thing I have ever had to go through".

The views expressed by the parents in these private disputes strikingly echo those of parents involved in public law cases (Freeman and Hunt, 1998). Thus, they spoke of feeling "isolated", "belittled" and "on the defensive". They were upset and/or angry because they had not been able to get their point of view across or had not been listened to:

> "I felt isolated; viciously attacked and belittled by her barrister. The judge would not allow the issue of shared residence to be raised in court; I felt always on the defensive." (Father)

> "Because you can't answer what they're saying at the time I felt I wasn't able to put my views forward. He was spouting a load of rubbish in court, [but] you can't say, you have to wait. And I didn't really get a chance to talk to my barrister about what he was saying so I didn't really get a chance to counter [it]." (Mother)

In general, even those expressing more positive views were not gainsaying these perceptions. Rather they appeared to be reflecting their own satisfaction with the way their side of the case had gone, especially if this had been contrary to their expectations:

> "The hearing went well – all her lies came out – she was still drinking and her new partner was violent." (Father)

> "Both [father] and his new partner were told that they were so negative towards me that it wasn't surprising that I wanted to get away from them; that was the judge that said that. It made me feel that at least I wasn't the only one who was feeling this. I've had a lot of people say to me, 'Well, no, that's not quite the case, I think you're going a bit over the top here', so to hear somebody else say exactly the same was nice." (Mother)

Thirteen fathers and eleven mothers reported giving evidence and/or being cross-examined. A few parents had not found this too uncomfortable an experience. Indeed, three fathers seem to have positively enjoyed it:

> "Me? I loved it. I was able to say what I wanted to, very much so. I felt actually her barrister fumbled, they wanted to have me up there to get at me. They tried different questions and the judge actually said, 'You've asked that question three different ways and he has answered. Are you not satisfied?'" (Father)

However, a large proportion of parents were very negative about the experience which they variously described, again as did the parents in Freeman's study (Freeman and Hunt, 1998), as "intimidating", "scary", "frightening", making them feel de-humanised, belittled or treated like a criminal:

> "I was interrogated for four hours; my reputation was dragged through the sewer. His barrister went on and on, twisted everything to discredit me; said things to make me angry: 'Your child doesn't want to live with you'. I would like to kill her [the barrister] – there's no need for gratuitous cruelty – it was like on TV, but this is real life and people get badly hurt." (Mother)

> "I can remember it feeling really frightening, that the wall was coming out at me; I didn't like it. I didn't like the way there was a dock. If we'd all been sitting round one table. I felt I was in the dock and there was this man facing you that you don't get on with at all. You felt you were on trial." (Mother)

> "There was so much overt aggression from her barrister – you wouldn't put a dog through it." (Father)

Some parents also vividly recalled being physically affected by the experience. One mother described herself as "trembling, feeling sick". Another, who had to face cross-examination by her unrepresented and reportedly violent ex-partner, said:

> "I was terrified. I got to the point where they were saying would I like a chair or a glass of water. I was in a terrible state. It was because it was him asking the questions. Old habits die hard; I found standing up to him very difficult." (Mother)

Nor, it seems, was the trauma of the court experience necessarily compensated for by the feeling that the hearing had been fair and thorough. Of the parents who expressed an opinion, less than a half were satisfied that the court knew enough about their family to make a decision, and only just over a third that they had had a fair hearing. Moreover, while perceptions of fairness were statistically related to outcome, views about thoroughness were not. There was no statistically significant difference by gender.

In the 'couple' cases, it was striking that diametrically opposed views dominated: four of seven couples disagreeing totally on whether the hearing had been fair and five of six on whether the court knew enough about the family to make a decision. On both issues there was no difference by gender.

Views about the court process

Criticism of the court proceedings was not confined to those who had gone to a contested hearing. Asked to identify aspects of the court process that they had found helpful or unhelpful, only one in ten parents expressed entirely positive views compared to six out of ten who were entirely negative. The rest thought the process was neither helpful nor unhelpful, with some identifying both positive and negative aspects of the process. There was no difference between mothers and fathers.

Sixty parents responded to a question asking them to rate the quality of service they had received from the court. These responses tended to be rather more positive: a third rating the service as either excellent or good, just over a third as average and nearly another third as poor. The highest proportion of positive ratings were for cases heard in the High Court, followed by those in the family proceedings courts with the county courts trailing behind. More than a third of parents rated the service provided in the county courts as poor.

What did parents find *helpful* about the court process? Given the predominantly negative views expressed the data is necessarily scanty. Of the 13 items mentioned, just five were mentioned by more than one respondent and only one – the approach of the judge

Table 3.3: What parents found unhelpful about the court process (number of comments)

Delay	14
Approach of the judge	8
Inappropriateness of the process	5
Inadequate coverage/lack of understanding of the issues	5
The system	4
Judicial discontinuity	4
Trauma of court	4
Lack of control by the court	3
Inefficiency	3

– by more than three. The material is much richer in relation to what parents found to be unhelpful, although again only a few points were made by more than one or two respondents (Table 3.3).

It is striking that the 'approach of the judge' emerges as an important factor in both categories, as it did in the Freeman study (Freeman and Hunt, 1998). Moreover, 26 parents identified this as one of the most (11) or least (15) helpful aspects of the court process.

"The judge was very, very experienced. I credit him with being very wise. He was paying meticulous attention to everything that was being said." (Father)

"It would be helpful to see the same judge, if you actually believed that the judge had read the papers before you went in – I was pretty much convinced they hadn't.... They're dealing with people's lives, there's a chance you'll lose your kids – they should at least look acquainted with the case." (Mother)

Fourteen parents identified *delay* as one of the least helpful aspects of proceedings. In addition another 43 parents, responding to a specific question about duration, said that proceedings had gone on too long. Only 23 parents thought that proceedings had been about the right length, and one thought they had been too short. The majority opinion is reflected in the following comments:

"It should have been dealt with much more quickly; the courts are overloaded; they don't have the capacity." (Father)

"I found it very slow. There's no one saying, 'It should be here within that time, it must be done'; they can always get extensions to time. It's, 'no, I can't do this', 'I can't do that', 'let's put it off for a month'. And it's put off twice; it's put off three times. Nobody is saying 'no'. There is no control." (Father)

A few parents commented that, although the proceedings were long, either this was necessary, or in the end the delay had a positive effect. For the most part, however, parents saw delay as damaging, referring to the stress on themselves, the children, and their partners and children in their new family, using words such as "agony", "going through hell" and "cruel".

"It's hanging over you like a black cloud all the time. I was crossing off the calendar every week; I couldn't plan, book a holiday, decide anything. Everything was in limbo; that date was like a big brick wall." (Mother)

"Delay led to a great deal of stress and anxiety, leading to problems in the relationship with my new partner." (Father)

What parents had to say was, again, strikingly reminiscent of the views expressed by parents in public law proceedings. Both groups highlight the importance of the emphasis in the Children Act on the avoidance of delay and the sad fact that, as yet, the legislation has had only limited effect (Hunt et al, 1999).

Impact of the court process on parents

Delay serves to prolong and amplify the effects of a process that is intrinsically highly stressful. Although a small number of parents said the proceedings had had a negligible impact on them, and one father actually found it a positive, empowering experience, the vast majority described a disruptive, nerve-wracking and exhausting process which came to dominate their lives and adversely affected their psychological and physical health.

The distress described by interviewees was reflected in their responses to standardised tests with 84% of parents completing the GHQ showing levels above the normal range (see Chapter 8). The capacity of parents suffering such high levels of stress to cope with the ordinary tasks of childrearing, let alone to support children who were themselves distressed, is likely to have been severely compromised through the proceedings. As will be seen in Chapter 8, many of the children were indeed exhibiting a high level of distress.

Summary

- The majority of cases ended with an order being made. Two in five were in favour of the applicant.
- Two in five of all parents were completely satisfied with the outcome of proceedings and a fifth entirely dissatisfied.
- Black parents were particularly dissatisfied with the outcome of the proceedings (only 15% were satisfied) and parents *without* high levels of distress (normal GHQ scores) or where domestic violence was *not* an issue were particularly satisfied (60%). Differences between other groups of parents were not marked.
- A third of cases were settled before the court hearing, a third at the door of the court and a third required adjudication. Parents who settled before the day of the court hearing were most satisfied with the outcome, those who went to adjudication the least satisfied. The same pattern obtained for satisfaction with the process.
- Almost all parents were critical about the court process. Most found the experience extremely stressful and participation at a final hearing particularly distressing.

4

The parents' experiences

The role of the FCWO is to inquire professionally and impartially into the circumstances of each case in order to discover information likely to assist the court in reaching decisions which are in the best interest of the child. He or she will report what they see and hear, offer the court their assessment of the situation and, where appropriate, make a recommendation. Questions of residence and contact always have to be considered on the merits of the individual case, in light of all the relevant circumstances, but ultimately it is for the Judge to decide on these questions, taking into account all the evidence placed before them. (CAFCASS, 2001, 'Frequently asked questions', at www.cafcass.gov.uk/faq.htm)

Overwhelmingly, parents believed that their experiences of welfare reporting needed to be heard and they welcomed the opportunity to talk to a researcher. They described an important, and often distressing, event in their lives and their children's lives, and they wanted their views brought to the attention of practitioners, the judiciary and policy makers.

Three features of the interviews stood out. First, many parents spoke of their experiences with great depth and strength of feeling. Many described anger, bitterness, betrayal, frustration and anxiety. Others talked of being supported and understood. Second, their views were extremely diverse. There was not a single question in the long interviewing schedule that prompted a unanimous answer. The accounts that mothers and fathers gave of the same events were sometimes dramatically different. Finally, it was clear that the preparation of the welfare report is a dynamic event for parents in that, for many, their views about the process changed over time.

Preconceptions

Parents arrive at the door of the FCWO with varying degrees of knowledge about how a welfare report is prepared. Forty-five parents already had first-hand experience, as a welfare report had previously been prepared on their child. Many had strong feelings about their own and their child's involvement.

Figure 4.1 gives an overview of how different groups of parents in different circumstances felt about the ordering of the welfare report, giving the percentage of those who felt 'entirely positive'. Among those most positive about the ordering of the welfare report were applicant non-resident fathers at the bottom of the figure (especially when compared to their 'opposite' respondent resident mothers – fifth bar down); those who were coming to the court for the first time; black parents (see Appendix B for a discussion of grouping issues); those on Income Support; and those mothers for whom fear or domestic violence was not an issue in the proceedings.

Figure 4.1: Parental attitude to the ordering of the welfare report

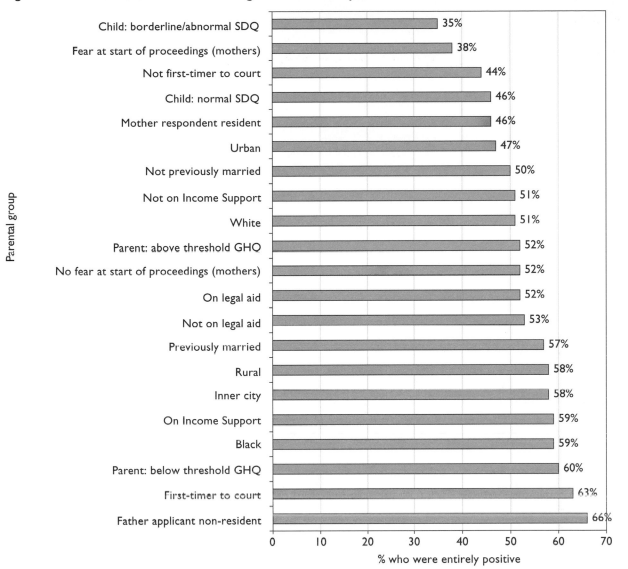

Note: GHQ = General Health Questionnaire; SDQ = Strengths and Difficulties Questionnaire.

Why parents were positive about the ordering of the welfare report

- Predominantly, they had instigated the proceedings.
- They saw the report as a means of achieving their objectives.
- They wanted someone else to see what was going on and make sure that the children were all right.
- They wanted a neutral outsider to intervene in a painful dispute which they were unable to settle unaided.
- They saw the welfare report as an opportunity to put their side of the case or vindicate their position.

What positive parents said

"I was hopeful that it would get contact established." (Mother)

"I was confident that it would be an independent report." (Father)

"The children would be more open with an outsider." (Father)

"I wanted to put on record my side. My ex-partner had maligned me as a schizophrenic and incompetent. The Family Court Welfare Officer had got a lot of experience with children and separation and would be helpful." (Mother)

> ### Why parents did not want a welfare report
>
> - They were predominantly respondents.
> - They felt they were forced into the process against their will.
> - They did not wish their child to be involved in the adults' conflict.
> - They believed the application was without foundation.
> - They felt powerless, abused and distressed.
> - They thought they would be checked up on.
> - They had previous poor experience of a welfare report being prepared.

> ### What negative parents said
>
> "I was outraged, angry and upset. I didn't want [child] to be involved – he was too young. I was worried in case he would be upset. I wanted to protect him from the conflict." (Mother)
>
> "I was absolutely devastated. You hear these things. You think, God, someone is going to go to your children's school and come to your house, and who knows what they are going to find out? You think of social workers and all those horrible things – child abuse." (Mother)

Before they met the FCWO for the first time, some parents described conflicting hopes, fears and anxiety about the outcome.

> "I hoped that there would be no contact but feared that [child] would be forced, against her wishes, to see her father." (Mother)
>
> "I hoped to see the children but feared that there would be no chance." (Father)

Some parents were frightened because they did not know what to expect or because they feared the worst, for example 'losing' their child or imprisonment, should they oppose the court decision.

First impressions

Information and understanding of the role

Even before they were contacted by the FCWO, most parents said that they had a good understanding of the FCWO's role. This had been explained to them by their solicitor, the court, or they had had past experience of a welfare report being prepared. Only six parents said that they had not received written information from the FCWS before they met the FCWO. None of the 19 parents whose first language was not English said that they had received written material in any language except English. Three parents could not understand the written material sent to them: they represent a small proportion of the sample but for these parents a translation was essential to enable them to participate in the process.

From the ordering of the welfare report to the first interview

Parents were, on the whole, very unclear about how long they had to wait before they met the FCWO for the first time; 60% said they thought it was over a month. The majority, however, regarded the interval as reasonable.

The first interview

Parents enter the office of the FCWO experiencing a wide range of emotions; half said that they were anxious or apprehensive, a third were positive and one in six were hostile.

Why parents were anxious and apprehensive

- They believed that the decision about their children would be heavily influenced by how the meeting went.
- They were anxious because they were in a new situation.
- They worried that they needed to make a good impression.
- They thought they would be judged.

What anxious and apprehensive parents said

"I was nervous. I had never been involved with the police or court before. It was completely new. I didn't want to mess up." (Mother)

"It was so important – wondering if I should be honest about everything that happened." (Mother)

"I was terrified, shaking. I was afraid that she would assess my character and level criticism at me for being a working mother." (Mother)

Why parents were hostile

- They already had negative experiences of a welfare report being prepared.
- They objected to the welfare report being prepared.

What hostile parents said

"Here I go again having to justify why I don't think extended contact is right for children when it's taken me three years to settle their routine." (same FCWO as previous welfare report) (Mother)

"The process shouldn't have been taking place at all. I didn't need this intrusion in my life. It seemed pointless, petty and a waste of time." (Mother)

Why parents were hopeful

- They expected the FCWO to understand what they had been going through.
- They were confident of the strength of their case.
- They had had a good experience previously.
- They expected the FCWO to support their position.

What hopeful parents said

"I was hopeful. Somebody might see a way forward that others hadn't seen." (Father)

The end of the first meeting

The first meeting with the FCWO was a critical one for parents. It was the first key point in the dynamic process that took place when a welfare report was prepared. They learnt about the person who would be advising the court on their child's future, how the investigation would be done and the criteria they would be using to make the assessment. Most parents left the first meeting with the FCWO with their attitudes and feelings changed by the experience. For many the impact was profound; hopes were dashed or anxieties were allayed.

A quarter of parents who had been positive about the ordering of the welfare report said that they felt worse when they left the first interview. Nearly half of the parents who had negative feelings about the ordering of the welfare report reported that they felt better at the end of the first meeting. For parents who were neutral or had mixed feelings about the ordering of the report, the first interview was generally a reassuring experience.

Some parents had their initial feelings confirmed at the first meeting. Of the parents who were positive at the start, nearly two thirds described themselves as feeling better after first meeting the FCWO. Nearly half of those who were negative had these feelings

Figure 4.2: Change in parents' feelings after the first meeting with the FCWO (*n*=100)

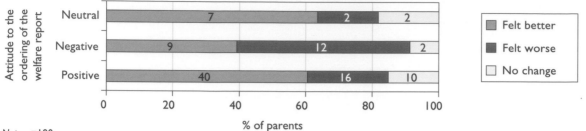

Note: *n*=100.

reinforced. The reasons why parents' feelings and views may have changed will be examined in the next chapter.

Parents were asked to describe how the welfare report had been prepared. Some remembered the process with greater clarity than others. No checks were made to establish whether or not the parents' recollections about practice were accurate or not.

Role of the FCWO

Four out of five parents were satisfied with how the FCWO had explained their role. With the exception of one parent, who was only interviewed over the telephone for a supplementary report, all the sample parents saw the FCWO at least once. Four out of five parents said they met the FCWO on two or more occasions. Only one in five said that their ex-partner had been present at one of these meetings. Thirteen parents were never interviewed on their own. This is a very different picture from that described by James and Hay (1993) who did their research at the end of the 1980s when both parents were seen together in about two out of three cases. There was little evidence from the parents that FCWOs worked with colleagues: 11% said that a second FCWO had been present at one of the interviews. Over half the parents said that the FCWO had not visited their home.

Interviews with children

Five parents (four cases) said that their children had not been seen by a FCWO. The other parents (95%) said that their child had been seen at least once. A total of 70% of parents were seen on at least one occasion with their child. Resident and non-resident

parents were equally likely to be seen with their children. Only 5% of parents described a meeting that involved the child, the interviewee and the ex-partner.

Again this is a very different picture of practice than that described by James and Hay (1993) and in the inspection report into family court welfare work (HM Inspectorate of Probation, 1997), which both reported a higher proportion of cases in which children were not seen.

Who else did the FCWO talk to?

In order to carry out their investigations, FCWOs routinely contact other professionals, such as teachers and health visitors, and may speak to other family members. In this study, 35 parents said that the FCWO had been in touch either directly or on the telephone with other members of their family, their ex-partner's family, friends or neighbours; 64 parents reported no contact with other family members. Sixty-one said that the FCWO had been in touch with another professional; 20 said that they had not contacted another professional; 15 did not know.

A large proportion of parents were unclear about who the FCWO had in fact contacted and whether social services and criminal record checks had been done.

Differing practices by area

At the time the research was undertaken, all FCWSs were required to adhere to national standards for family court welfare work (Home Office, 1994). However, these were not prescriptive about the details of practice. James and Hay (1993), whose research covered six FCWS teams, described very

Figure 4.3: Family and professionals contacted by the FCWO*

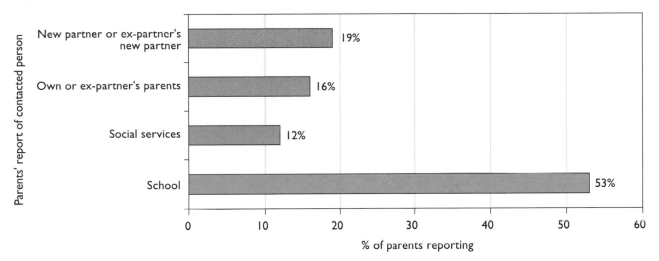

Note: * Categories not mutually exclusive.

Figure 4.4: Time taken from ordering of report to first interview: less than one month

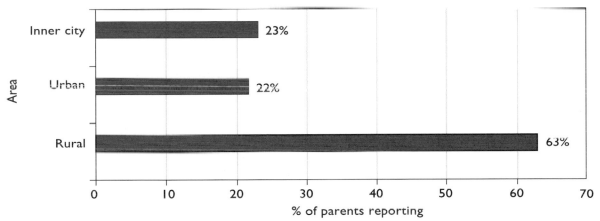

Note: n−59.

Figure 4.5: Home visits by area: at least one

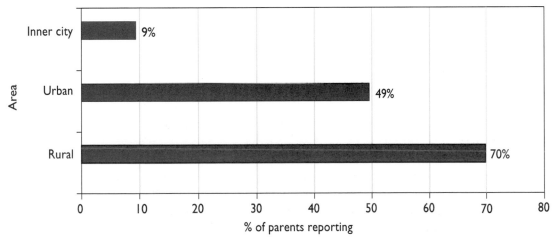

Note: n=88.

different practices in relation to home visiting, coworking, interviews with both parents present and whether or not children were seen. The accounts of the parents from the three different areas in this study confirm that different approaches are still used in the preparation of a welfare report. The main variations occurred in the length of time FCWOs took to arrange the first interview, home visiting, coworking and the number of times children were seen by the FCWO. The ethnic background of parents did not affect their account of practice nor did the presence of domestic violence.

Parents from the rural area in this study said that the first interview was arranged more quickly than for parents in the other two areas.

In the rural area, far fewer parents said that they felt worse after the first meeting (18%) than in the inner-city (48%) and urban (41%) areas.

Home visiting and coworking were the practices that most clearly differentiated the three areas. FCWOs in the rural area were much more likely to have undertaken a home visit than those in the inner–city area.

There was an even greater discrepancy in relation to coworking. Over a third of the inner-city parents said that two FCWOs had been present at one or more of the interviews, while only one parent reported coworking in the urban area and no parents reported this happening in the rural area.

As would be expected from the differences in the level of home visiting, children were usually seen at home in the rural area but only exceptionally in the inner-city area. In the rural area the FCWO was said to see the child on more occasions than in the other two areas (see Figure 4.5).

Although most parents had an opportunity to read the welfare report, for various reasons three chose not to and one mother could not remember if she had seen it. Most (89%) saw it after it had been filed but before the court hearing. All the parents who saw their report were given a copy to keep.

Preparation of the welfare report

The influence of the FCWO

Most parents believed that the welfare report carried great weight with the judge or magistrate who would be deciding on their child's future. Parents saw the FCWO's assessment of the children's needs and of their own capacity to meet those needs as critically important. Only six parents said that they thought the FCWO had little influence; the other parents believed that the FCWO did make a difference.

> "It's strange that a stranger could come into your life and, in a couple of weeks, change your life forever." (Mother)

Satisfaction with the process

Parents were not asked directly about their overall satisfaction with the preparation of the welfare report; however, they were assessed by the researchers as being satisfied, mainly satisfied, mainly dissatisfied or dissatisfied. Their responses were based on answers to a range of questions about various elements in the process:

- how the investigation was conducted;
- the attitude and skills of the FCWO;
- how their children were involved;
- the content of the welfare report.

Figure 4.6 shows that 56% of parents were not satisfied with the overall process of the welfare report preparation. In the next chapter some of the underlying reasons which might explain why parents were either satisfied or dissatisfied will be considered.

The investigation

Parents' views about how the FCWO carried out the investigation varied greatly. Their evaluations, both of the FCWO's skills and attitudes and of the details of practice, were often mixed, but for many parents they were relentlessly critical. Inevitably, parents who were disappointed or frustrated with the process tended to express their feelings more strongly than those who were satisfied. Dissatisfied parents tended to be critical of the attitudes and skills of the FCWO and of the arrangements made for the investigation. Satisfied

Figure 4.6: Parental satisfaction with preparation of the welfare report

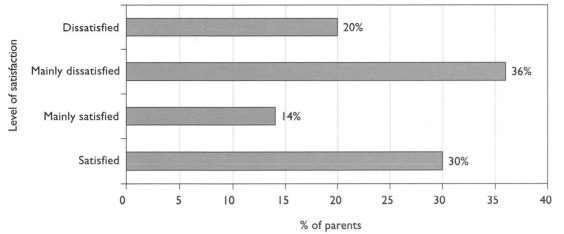

Note: *n*=100.

parents concentrated on the FCWO's attitudes and skills and had less to say about the time devoted to the investigation or the people seen.

Time

The criticism voiced most frequently was that FCWOs had insufficient time to spend with parents and children. Half expressed dissatisfaction, 36% were satisfied and 14% had no view.

> **Not enough time**
>
> "I thought she would be coming to our home once a week ... spend some time with the children and understand and try to unravel it." (Mother)
>
> "I don't know how the FCWO can make a decision after one hour." (Father)
>
> "There was not enough time. I could have been a good liar." (Mother)

Involving the family

Similarly, half the parents said that they did not think that the FCWO got to know their family well enough to write the welfare report. They were often surprised that new partners or grandparents had not been approached: 27 interviewees said that they had a partner who was living in the home with them, 11 of these said that their new partner had been contacted by the FCWO. Nine parents said that they would

have liked their new partner to be interviewed; 14 mentioned other family members who they thought should have been interviewed, for example the child's aunts and uncles, or older siblings. Five parents went beyond the family and suggested that the FCWO should have contacted friends, neighbours or even employers.

Generally, these parents wanted family and friends involved because they believed that this would give the FCWO a better picture of the child. Sometimes they argued that, since the FCWO had seen the ex-partner's new partner or parents, as a matter of fairness their own should be seen too.

> **Did not get to know the family well enough**
>
> "It would have been appropriate for her to see my new partner. [Child] has known her for 10 years and is extremely close to her. She has been living with us for over a year. She talks more to her stepmother than to me." (Father)
>
> "It's a good idea to talk to the grandparents. They are at one stage removed and have the children's interests at heart. They would corroborate certain things and wouldn't want to settle scores." (Father)
>
> "I have no family here. I would have liked the FCWO to talk to people who know how difficult it is for me to bring up a child on my own, people helping me, perhaps a letter from my employer and my ex-partner's sister who knows us both." (Mother)

"She saw the paternal grandparents. She should have seen my parents too." (Mother)

Some of the parents who were disappointed that other family members were not interviewed also recognised that family members may take sides.

Taking sides
"It's complicated. She would get different stories from each side of the family." (Father)

"Everyone's in a camp." (Mother)

Contact with other professionals

As with the FCWO's contacts with family members, parents were more dissatisfied about the professionals who were not seen than about those who were.

Dissatisfied with professionals not seen
"More weight should have been given to the evidence from the social worker." (Father)

"She should have spoken to the head teacher to get a picture of what [child] has been like and how it has affected his behaviour at school, and she should have spoken to his teacher." (Father)

On the other hand some parents felt equally strongly that other professionals should not have been contacted, because it was irrelevant or because of embarrassment to the child. Two mothers objected to the school being contacted. Another parent commented that she did not understand why medical reports had been asked for. A mother was distressed during her interview with the FCWO to be asked about allegations of sexual abuse on an older child that had occurred 15 years previously; she regarded these allegations as irrelevant to the investigation on her two-year-old daughter.

Home visits

A frequently voiced criticism was that children were interviewed in the FCWS office and not in their home or that of the non-resident parent. Three quarters of the parents interviewed at the second stage of the research believed that a home visit should be done in every case. These parents argued that the

child ought to be seen on familiar territory: it is only at home that the child will feel comfortable; it is here that they can be understood and where their relationship with the adults in their life can be observed. These parents were worried that in the unfamiliar situation of an office the child's true nature would not be apparent and that they would be unable to express their views. For the non-resident parent a further problem with an office interview was that the child was invariably brought to the premises by the resident parent, which they believed put them at a disadvantage.

The premises

Nearly half the parents commented on the premises of the FCWSs. Parents in the rural area were notably more complimentary about the premises than parents in the inner city. The urban area came in between.

"It was horrible. It was badly equipped for children and adults. It was forbidding and poorly decorated and frightening for children. The toys were too young for a nine-year-old." (Mother)

"It was visibly the offices of the probation service, quasi-criminal. It was an awful office, intimidating. You have failed as a parent." (Father)

The parents who were broadly satisfied with the arrangements made for carrying out the investigation had little to say about time and place. They concentrated on the interaction between themselves, their children and the FCWO, and the skill with which the FCWO carried out their role, which will be considered later in this chapter (see pages 38-40).

Seeing the children

Parents were divided in their assessment of the FCWO's direct contact with their child. Sixty per cent said that they agreed with the principle of the FCWO seeing their child and half the parents had no reservations about the arrangements actually made (Figure 4.7). Parents also had different views about the number of times their children were seen.

Five parents who said that the FCWO had not seen their children, supported the decision as it had been

Figure 4.7: Parents' attitude to the FCWO's arrangements to see their children

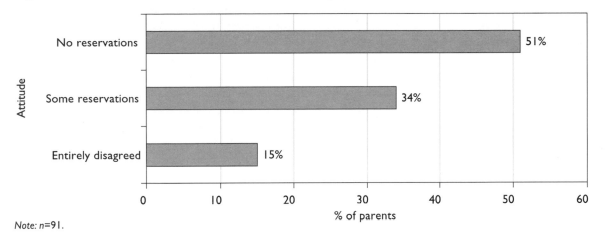

Note: n=91.

Figure 4.8: Parents' feelings about how often the children were seen

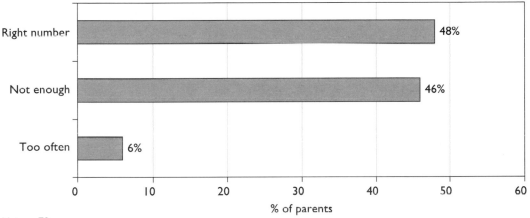

Note: n=78.

taken jointly. There was a small number of parents who believed that the children should not have been seen but who felt forced to agree to an interview. In their view, the child was too young to be involved in an adult dispute of which they claimed the child was unaware.

Parents who expressed reservations about the contact the FCWO had with their child were worried for a variety of reasons. They expressed concerns about the level of skill of the FCWO in interviewing children and assessing their needs and views. Some said they were concerned by the techniques used by the FCWO with children, such as asking children to score out of ten their feelings about those people close to them. Parents worried that FCWOs were unable to distinguish between a child's real feelings and those foisted on them by the other, usually resident, parent. They believed that the FCWO gave

too much weight to the child's views and therefore too much responsibility to the child for the decision. The suggestion was made that the FCWO should spend more time getting to know the child and that the investigation should be more relaxed and child-friendly. Two parents believed that the FCWO concentrated on the views of the older child, neglecting the needs of the younger.

Two mothers were very angry that, in their view, their children were used as 'guinea-pigs' in the court process. One mother complained that contact had been set up so that the father could demonstrate a change in behaviour. She felt that his ability to control his heavy drinking should have been assessed independently of contact sessions with the children.

The parents who were comfortable with the arrangements and, indeed, those who had some reservations believed that it was important that their child was seen and allowed to talk to a neutral person. It was also important that the child was listened to and that their views carried weight. In some instances children had been helped by the FCWO to talk to a parent about what they wanted.

Listening to children

"She enabled the children to talk about their feelings about their father." (Mother)

"She made it very clear that [child's] wishes should be taken into account." (Father)

Working with children

"She was lovely with the kids. She didn't patronize them. They loved it. She was very astute." (Mother)

"She was fantastic. She was so careful with the children – how she spoke to them, what she said." (Mother)

The FCWO's attitudes and skills

Satisfied parents

As Figure 4.9 shows, almost half the parents were confident that the FCWO understood their feelings and views.

What was helpful?

- Being put at their ease and reassured.
- Being listened to.
- Knowledge of family dynamics.
- Enabling parents to reevaluate their positions.
- Focus on the interests of the child.
- Helpful advice.
- Help in thinking about what would be best for the child.
- Neutrality and professionalism.
- Help in enabling the parents to talk about their children.
- Accessibility.

What positive parents said

"She listened. It wasn't like talking to a brick wall. She was really nice and had some useful insights. It was helpful to talk to someone." (Mother)

"Her advice [was helpful] really because she had seen so many of these situations before." (Father)

"She was objective. She didn't have preformed ideas." (Father)

"She was good at her job. She did everything well." (Mother)

"She helped me become more realistic about what I could achieve." (Father)

"She managed to get us to talk to each other and reach an agreement." (Father)

Parents noted when the FCWO's influence led to a change in arrangements that they wanted.

"I got evening visits as well as weekends." (Father)

"She made a lot of difference. She advised times and dates for the contact and managed to get us to talk to each other." (Father)

Dissatisfied parents

Dissatisfied parents were not only critical of the way the investigation was conducted, they frequently had strong and negative views about the attitude and professionalism of the FCWO, with over a third of parents making critical observations.

Figure 4.9: Parents' attitudes as to whether the FCWO understood their feelings and views

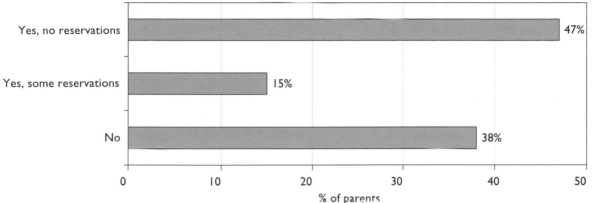

Note: *n*=100.

What was not helpful?

- When the investigation felt like a routine matter and the individuality of the family was not taken into account.
- Not feeling listened to or understood.
- Taking no account of the history of the parental relationship.
- Taking no account of a parent's failure to act responsibly towards their child, or their lack of interest.
- A sense of being betrayed by the FCWO if their attitude appeared to change.
- Lack of neutrality and professionalism.
- Being judged or criticised.

What critical parents said

"I felt like a number – when 'phoning I was asked for my case number and not my name." (Father)

"She wasn't there to help you. I know she is there for the child but that is not enough. It was so impersonal. She didn't care. She was like a robot." (Mother)

"She ignored many of my concerns in writing the report." (Mother)

"She was very pleasant, personable and objective, but I didn't ever feel that she appreciated the situation I had been in and my real concerns for [child]." (Mother)

"I asked her if she had read our statements. She said, 'Yes, but I'm not a historian'. So our statements were irrelevant. What's the point? Our past is relevant to now." (Mother)

"She didn't want to know about the past. So she missed the whole picture." (Father)

"I wish she had been more honest with me. Then I would have known not to use her for support." (Mother)

"She was unprofessional and not impartial. She was economical with fact finding and allowed herself to be manipulated by the father." (Mother)

"She was biased against me. She appeased the mother and fell for her ploys. She kept referring to 'father's contact' and not 'child's contact with father'." (Father)

"She treated me with coldness and suspicion, like how I imagine being interviewed by police. I was treated as if I was a criminal." (Father)

Figure 4.10: Parents' views on the welfare report*

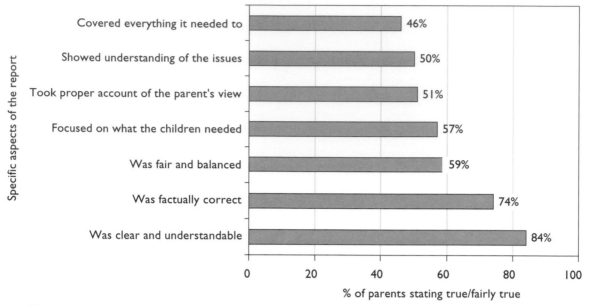

Note: *Categories not mutually exclusive.

A frequently voiced concern was that the FCWO had made up their mind at the outset and that their recommendation was a foregone conclusion. These parents saw decision making in private family law as formulaic rather than based on the needs of individual children. Most fathers believed that residence would always go to mothers and many mothers believed that an application for contact by a father guaranteed that contact would be ordered. These concerns that the FCWO, in effect, had a political agenda relating to residence and contact will be examined in greater depth in Chapter 9.

The welfare report

The first turning point for some parents was the first meeting with the FCWO. The second was when they read the welfare report. The national standards for family court welfare work (Home Office, 1994) make it clear that, "Court welfare officers should keep the parties informed of their thinking and emerging conclusions so that the final report does not hold any surprises (p 22)". Many parents, however, said that they were surprised, usually unpleasantly, by what they read in the welfare report. Reading a 'negative' report was a profoundly distressing experience.

"I was so shocked. All my concerns were dismissed. It was a totally glowing report about [ex-partner]. I felt so helpless I just screamed and screamed." (Mother)

"I was shocked at the impression she had got. She had made up her mind and then found evidence to support it." (Father)

"I felt worthless when I read it." (Mother)

A few parents, however, were pleasantly surprised when they read the welfare report:

"It was a good report, more objective than last time – a complete reversal. She favoured us more than [child's] mother. It's funny – she came across one way and then you see the report and it's different. Well-worded." (Father)

The content of the report

The national standards (Home Office, 1994) provide guidance on the qualities that should be found in all welfare reports. Parents were asked if they did or did not find these qualities in the reports.

Figure 4.11: Parents' concerns and subsequent action*

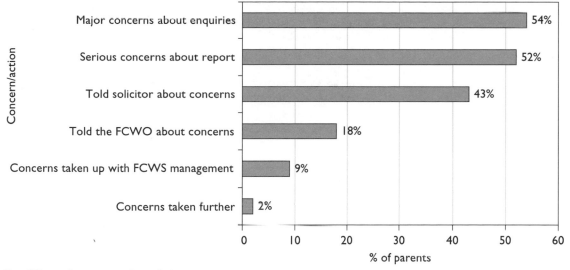

Note: *Categories not mutually exclusive.

As Figure 4.10 shows, most reports were described as clear, understandable and factually accurate. Parents were less satisfied with the way reports dealt with the substantive issues, with only 46% believing that it covered everything it needed to and 59% that it was fair and balanced. Parents who were critical of the welfare report said that the issues were covered in a superficial way, that key issues were not addressed or that the parent's own views were misrepresented. On the other hand, there were parents who were very satisfied with the report.

> **Parents' views on the report**
>
> "It was very poor. It did not address the critical issue of how contact could be more positive for the child." (Mother)
>
> "I have no grievances. I was pleased with what was written. Everything I wanted was there. It made the decision much clearer so that more weight could be applied to the court." (Father)

There were 23 cases in which both parents gave their views on the quality of the welfare report. In just over half of the cases one parent viewed the report favourably and the other was critical. In around a quarter, the parents agreed about some elements but disagreed about others. In three cases both parents took a positive view of the report and in one case both viewed the report critically.

Children in the reports

Focusing on the children's needs in the report does not in itself make it an adequate document in parents' eyes. More parents said that the report focused on the children's needs than believed that it covered everything it needed to. Most of the 78 parents who had children old enough to have their views reported said that these had been addressed in the report and over half were satisfied with how this was done.

The recommendation

A total of 84% of parents said that a recommendation had been made in the welfare report. Although parents were not asked if they knew what the recommendation would be, it was clear that a number did not. The discovery could be extremely distressing. Either parents had not been kept informed of the FCWO's thinking, as is required by the national standards (Home Office, 1994), or they had not understood what they were being told. Nine parents said either that they had been told what the recommendation would be or that they had been able to infer it.

Parents' views on the recommendation

"I had no indication of the recommendation before the report was filed. I was amazed the FCWO had listened to [child]. The recommendation was what he wanted." (Mother)

"I didn't know what the FCWO was going to say beforehand and was quite shocked that she recommended alternate weekends." (Mother)

"I had already gauged that she wouldn't be recommending residence [for me]." (Father)

"The FCWO had told me after her interview with [child] that she would be recommending contact [with mother] only if she wants it." (Father)

Dealing with dissatisfaction

As has been seen, there was a considerable dissatisfaction among parents, both with the way the FCWO conducted their enquiries and with the welfare report itself.

However, very few parents – three mothers and five fathers – made a complaint. One mother had got her solicitor to write about factual errors in the report, although she thought that it had had little effect. The other seven parents were concerned about the process. Three parents asked for a change of FCWO, each unsuccessfully. One father said that he had been offered a meeting with the Senior FCWO at which the FCWO he was objecting to was also present. The Senior FCWO argued that it would be in the child's best interests for the current worker to remain; the father had accepted her argument although subsequently regretted not insisting on a change. Only two parents took their complaints beyond the Senior FCWO. No parent who complained to the FCWS management seems to have obtained any sense of satisfaction, redress or benefit from taking this action. Parents who did not take up with the FCWS management what, to them, were serious concerns, appeared to feel that it would be a waste of time because either nothing would change or their case might even be jeopardised.

Summary

- Many parents were highly anxious about the first meeting with the FCWO, which was often critical, in that they left the meeting with their attitude to the process changed.
- Parents reported different practices in different areas.
- A total of 96% of the children were seen by the FCWO. Parents were divided in their views about the arrangements made to see the children and how well their wishes and feelings were reported.
- The main criticism made by parents was that the investigation was not thorough enough, both in the amount of time spent and the number of professionals and other family members who were contacted.
- Reading a 'negative' report was a very distressing experience for parents.

5

Differing perspectives

There has been a lot of criticism of the role Family Court Welfare Officers play ... and there are many people (especially fathers) who are unhappy with the decisions that have been made in the reports provided by FCWOs. It has been claimed that these officers spend little or no time at all with the child concerned and that they don't spend time finding out the needs of the family. (CAFCASS, 2001, 'Frequently asked questions', at www.cafcass.gov.uk/ faq.htm)

In the last chapter, parents gave very different accounts of having a welfare report prepared on their child. In this chapter, the possible reasons that might help to explain these differences will be examined. Were particular characteristics such as gender or ethnicity significant? Did the issue of domestic violence or concerns about childcare affect how they felt? What part did parents' expectations at the outset play, and did their feelings about the outcome have an influence?

As in previous chapters, the overall measure of satisfaction with the preparation of the report was analysed by the different parental categories (see Appendix A for the full definitions). For example, at the bottom of Figure 5.1 are parents whose children had a normal SDQ at the first interview, that is, did not have significant emotional or behavioural problems. Towards the top of the figure (the fourth bar down) are parents whose children did have such difficulties.

In Chapter 4 it was shown that only 44% of parents were satisfied or mainly satisfied (Figure 4.6). Interestingly, Figure 5.1 shows that levels of dissatisfaction did not vary greatly between groups. Only three groups (parents who were themselves not abnormally stressed, whose children had 'normal' SDQ scores or who were not on legal aid) showed

satisfaction levels of more than 50%. At the other end of the scale were parents who had not previously been married to each other.

Gender

Although the overall satisfaction of mothers and fathers was similar, their perceptions of and reactions to the process were different. This was particularly marked for parents, whether they were mothers or fathers, who had negative experiences.

The mothers' perspective

Mothers, who tended to be the resident parent and the respondent:

- resented the intervention of the court and FCWO in decisions about their child;
- felt that they knew better than an outsider what was in their child's best interests;
- felt that the family justice system was male-dominated and promoted the interests of the father against those of mother and child;
- saw the FCWO, usually a woman, as 'pro-father';
- argued that their own needs as carer were ignored;
- believed that fathers used the courts to continue an oppressive relationship from the past;
- believed that no account was taken of fathers' past failures to support and nurture their child;
- believed that the individual needs of their own child were sacrificed to the general principle that contact is in the interests of most children – a principle most did not dispute.

Figure 5.1: Parents' satisfaction with the welfare report process at the first interview

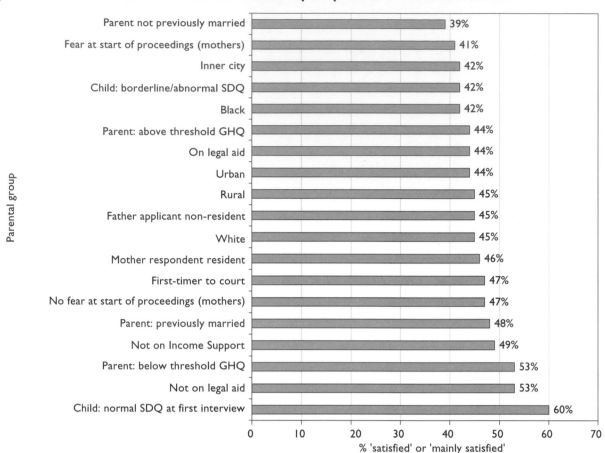

Note: GHQ = General Health Questionnaire; SDQ = Strengths and Difficulties Questionnaire.

The fathers' perspective

Fathers, who tended to be the applicant and non-resident parent:

- argued that their children's emotional well-being depended on a strong and positive relationship with both parents;
- felt that such a relationship could not be sustained or rebuilt unless the child spent a substantial amount of time in their company;
- believed that the small number of residence orders made in favour of fathers and the ineffective enforcement of contact orders demonstrated a systematic prejudice against fathers;
- saw the FCWO as an agent of the court and as adopting an 'anti-father' stance throughout their investigation;
- believed that FCWOs took the expressed wishes of their child at face value, ignoring the possibility that they had been heavily influenced by the mother.

A very much more positive view of the courts and the FCWS was taken by some women who felt supported in resisting their ex-partner's demands for extra contact. On the other hand, fathers who obtained greater or more regular contact as a result of the proceedings valued their FCWO's commitment to the principle that children benefited from knowing the non-resident parent. They saw the FCWO as taking their side against an intransigent ex-partner.

Gender of parent and gender of FCWO

Did parents regard the gender of the FCWO who was preparing the report as an important factor and, if they did, in what way? Of the 68 cases in which the gender of the FCWO was known, only eight were male. Many parents said that the gender of the FCWO was of no significance to them. However, it has to be noted that most of the mothers had female FCWOs, of which 14 said that this was important to them; they believed that their children would relate better to a woman than a man.

> "I felt more comfortable with her because she was a woman." (Mother)

Half the mothers who had male FCWOs felt this to be a disadvantage. One in particular said that it was difficult for her because of her experiences of domestic violence. No father made a positive comment about having a male FCWO, indeed, four fathers suggested that they preferred a female FCWO.

> "I would have chosen a woman if asked, but it was okay with a male FCWO." (Father)

One father who had a male FCWO said that he had expected him to be more sympathetic but had found this was not the case. Eight fathers would have preferred a male FCWO. Some men had found two women FCWOs in the interview particularly difficult to cope with and had interpreted this as a sign that the father's perspective would be automatically ignored.

> "The FCWO was biased against me because I am a man. She assumed [the ex partner's] account was correct and that domestic violence was still an issue." (Father)

One man, who admitted that he had been violent towards his ex-partner, was fearful that the FCWO would see only the woman's point of view.

The aspect of gender that mothers identified as important to them appeared to be motherhood rather than simply being a woman; nine women commented that it was important to them that a FCWO should be a mother. These mothers believed that only a FCWO who was a mother could assess what their own children needed and understand their own position. On the other hand, just one father said that he believed that it was important for the FCWO to be a parent. No parent mentioned the significance of a male FCWO being a father.

Five parents mentioned joint interviews in the context of gender issues. Four parents saw a joint interview by a male and female FCWO as a way of ensuring that neither parent was disadvantaged because of the gender of the FCWO. On the other hand, one father commented that having a male–female partnership in an interview had made no difference to the anti-father stance.

Ethnicity, race, religion and culture

As shown in Appendix B, the sample was highly diverse in terms of the parents' self-reported nationality, ethnic background and religion. Although 30% of the parents interviewed came from minority ethnic backgrounds, because of the small numbers involved in the subgroups, it was not possible to analyse parents' responses according to their ethnic or religious background. The only way to generate large enough numbers to make meaningful comparison possible was by grouping parents into those who broadly fell into the black population and those who broadly fell into the white population. It is recognised that this was a limitation in this study.

In spite of the diversity of the parents, of the 68 cases in which the ethnic background of the FCWO was known, only five were black. Five black parents, who all had a white FCWO, said that the difference in their ethnic background between them and the FCWO had mattered to them.

Figure 5.1 shows that, in terms of overall levels of satisfaction with the preparation of the welfare report, there were only three percentage points between the percentage of white parents and the percentage of black parents who were satisfied. There was, however, a tendency for black fathers to be more dissatisfied than white fathers and black mothers to be more satisfied than white mothers.

When asked to comment on aspects of their background that they believed needed to be taken into account in the preparation of the welfare report, half the black parents mentioned race or ethnicity, 43% mentioned culture and just over a quarter mentioned religion. Of these, 17% qualified their response by saying that they did not regard their own race and ethnicity, or that of their child, as relevant to the decision that needed to be made. Race, ethnicity, culture and religion were of far less significance to white parents. Only two white parents mentioned race, one mentioned religion and three culture.

Black parents made both positive and negative comments about the FCWO's approach to ethnicity, race, religion and culture.

Why parents were critical of the FCWO's approach to race, ethnicity, culture and religion

- A black FCWO would have assessed the ex-partner's claims about cultural differences more effectively than the white FCWO (two fathers).
- No effort was made to understand the cultural differences between the parents (two mothers).
- The religious concerns of a parent were ignored by the FCWO (two mothers).
- Contact was established on a day when the parent attended a religious service (mother).
- The FCWS systematically discriminated against black fathers (father).

What critical parents said

"Black women can make untrue claims about her culture and the father's culture. A black woman knows a black woman." (African-Caribbean father)

"I had to demonstrate more than a white father would have to. I had to make an effort to show that I am a worthy father." (African-Caribbean father)

Why parents were positive about the FCWO's approach to race, ethnicity, culture and religion

- A FCWO came to understand the father's position (even though it was different from the legal situation in England) (father).
- Black parents who held strong but different views on race, sexual orientation and religion, both commented that the FCWO had dealt with these issues openly and seriously (mother and father in the same case).
- The FCWO had discussed how the mother handled issues of race and culture with her child who was of mixed parentage (mother).
- The FCWO understood and respected cultural differences (mother).

What positive parents said

"First the FCWO was more on mother's side, then she understood my position. In the Indian way, children belong to the father; in UK the father only sees the children; but the law is the same for everyone." (Father)

"The FCWO was interested in cultural issues – she sought guidance from me." (Father)

Ethnicity and the welfare report

Although in terms of overall levels of satisfaction with the preparation of the welfare report there was little difference between white and black parents, Table 5.1 shows that black parents were less likely than white parents to feel that the welfare report covered everything it needed to.

What do these differences show? Did the white FCWOs fail to understand and convey issues relating to race, culture or religion? Or did the black parents' dissatisfaction relate to other issues?

Political correctness

Some parents thought that the FCWO had an agenda in relation to ethnicity and culture which they did not share or on which they would put different emphasis. These parents felt that the cultural and racial issues raised by the FCWO were not relevant to the decision that had to be made about the arrangements for the child.

Table 5.1: The report covered everything it needed to (% of parents)

	Black	White
True/fairly true	31	52
Not very true/not true	69	48

What parents said about political correctness

"The colour and race of a child are not important. You could have a green child and be parents." (Mother)

"Our Chinese family is close-knit, but cultural issues were not relevant to the decision about [child]." (Mother)

"There were no cultural issues of relevance, but the FCWO made issue of cultural differences between me and the children's [European] father. She was more concerned than I was, or the children. It was a political stance." (Mother)

Institutional racism?

The parents who were critical of the way the FCWO dealt with issues of race, ethnicity, culture and religion are a sharp reminder of how important sensitivity and a willingness to learn are in these areas. However, only one parent argued that his race had been a key factor in the decision not to give him residence.

"I am assertive but what about other black fathers? The FCWS is 95% against fathers and 100% against black fathers whose ex-partners are white women." (Black father)

Overall, however, the researchers were surprised by some positive views expressed by black parents. They had expected a greater sense of frustration and misunderstanding given the strong feelings in minority communities aroused by these issues, the identification of institutional racism in the police force (Home Office, 1999a) and the strongly-expressed belief of some parents that the FCWS was gender biased.

However, it should be noted that both interviewers were white, so it is possible that black parents had concerns about differential treatment or poor understanding of their background that they did not feel able to share.

Domestic violence

In recent years there has been growing concern both from outside and within the family justice system that the safety of women and their children has been jeopardised when decisions about residence and contact are made (see Chapter 1).

Critiques from research studies of FCWOs' approach to domestic violence

- FCWOs frequently failed to recognise and take proper account of domestic violence as a feature of contact and residence disputes.
- Mothers were put at risk because inadequate measures were taken to ensure their safety in the course of the welfare investigation.
- Mothers' views were not heard because they were interviewed with ex-partners and no account was taken of the imbalance of power.
- Dangerous contact arrangements could be made which exposed mothers and children to the risk of violence at handovers, or because a father was enabled to discover where the mother and children lived.
- The short- and long-term emotional effects on children of domestic violence were not understood and therefore not assessed when decisions about contact were made (see Hester and Radford 1996; Radford et al, 1999).

What did the parents in the sample think about how the issue of domestic violence was addressed by the family courts and the FCWS? The parents interviewed in stage 2 of the research were asked their views on the statements given in Table 5.2, which compared an ideal with the existing situation.

Mothers and fathers both believed that allegations of domestic violence should be taken seriously and they were both divided about the extent to which it was in fact taken seriously by the courts and FCWOs. The only significant divergence of view was on the appropriateness of accepting a parent's statement that domestic violence had occurred.

Some fathers were worried by messages about domestic violence, such as posters in waiting rooms, which they interpreted as a sign that the FCWS regarded all men as violent. They felt condemned as abusers before the investigation had started. There were also a few men who *had* been violent to their partners and who wanted to be honest, but feared that openness would result in blanket condemnation.

Violence or fear at the start of the proceedings

The extent of domestic violence in the research sample was explored in Chapter 2 where it was noted that, although it had been a feature of nearly four out of five relationships, by the time the proceedings started the proportion had dropped substantially. Nonetheless, at this stage there were still 28 cases (involving 24 mothers and 18 fathers) in which one parent, typically, but not invariably, the mother, was said to be afraid of their ex-partner.

There was a tendency for the fathers in these cases to be more satisfied with how the report was prepared than other fathers, but mothers for whom fear or violence was an issue at the start of the proceedings were less satisfied than other mothers (Figure 5.2).

It appeared to be difficult for some fathers to admit to being afraid or for them to ask the FCWO to take their accounts seriously. Nine men said that they had been the victims of their partner's violence and a further nine that there had been mutual violence. They could describe very serious violence against

themselves and yet deny its impact so far as they were concerned. On the other hand, some men believed that the violence they experienced was not given due weight by the FCWO.

> **A father who was critical of how domestic violence was addressed by the FCWO**
> Mr S said that his ex-partner had broken his nose and threatened him with knives. The police had been called to his parents' home where he had moved after separating. This father felt that his own account of the violence had not been believed by the FCWO although she had taken his ex-partner's experiences seriously.

Mothers for whom domestic violence was an issue in the proceedings

There were 11 mothers (21% of the mothers in the study) who were victims and who saw the violence of their partner as a factor to be considered during the preparation of the welfare report and in the decisions to be made about arrangements for their children. Three mothers opposed contact on principle and two wanted contact to be supervised; four contested the detail of the contact proposals and two were involved in residence applications. Two thirds of these mothers were not satisfied with the way in which the welfare report was prepared.

Table 5.2: Parents' views on domestic violence issues (not all parents answered every question)

		Agree	Sort of agree	Disagree
Ideal: Allegations of domestic violence should be taken very seriously	Mothers	32	1	0
	Fathers	29	5	1
What happens: The court/FCWO treat allegations of domestic violence very seriously	Mothers	11	3	13
	Fathers	15	3	10
Ideal: When a parent says domestic violence has taken place they should normally be believed	Mothers	17	13	6
	Fathers	10	8	19
What happens: Parents who allege domestic violence are normally believed	Mothers	12	1	12
	Fathers	13	7	8
Ideal: When there are active concerns about domestic violence the courts should start from the presumption that contact should be supervised	Mothers	31	3	4
	Fathers	23	3	10
What happens: When there are active concerns about domestic violence the courts do start from the presumption that contact should be supervised	Mothers	8	2	9
	Fathers	10	5	5

Only three out of the eleven felt that the FCWO had understood the situation and feelings about violence very well. Similarly, only three said that the FCWO had done anything to ensure their safety during the preparation of the report, while one mother said that her safety had been positively endangered. Another said that the actions of the FCWO had increased her safety in some respects and diminished it in others. Five felt that the FCWO had neither increased nor diminished their safety.

Of the nine mothers who stated whether or not they were satisfied with how the welfare report addressed the issue of domestic violence, five were not satisfied, one had some reservations and three were satisfied. Two mothers said (correctly) that the report had not mentioned domestic violence.

Mothers for whom domestic violence was an issue in the proceedings were more satisfied by the FCWO's arrangements to see the children than they were with the process overall: seven were comfortable with these arrangements, three had some reservations and one disagreed entirely with the arrangements made. Eight mothers said that their children had positive reactions after they had seen the FCWO and only one commented that her daughter became more distressed as the process went on ('as she got older').

Domestic violence and decision on contact

Domestic violence was an important issue for 11 mothers, seven of whom were not satisfied with the way in which the welfare report had been prepared. It was therefore very surprising that not one of these mothers believed that the decision about their child's contact or residence with the father should rest, either on the past violence that the mother had experienced and the child had witnessed, or on the possibility of violence occurring in the future.

These mothers did not deny the impact of the violence on either themselves or on their child, indeed, they believed that past and likely future violence were factors in the decision. However, they all advanced other and more pressing reasons for believing that contact should not take place or that the arrangements proposed by the father were not appropriate. They were primarily concerned about the father's inability to be a positive influence in their child's life. They also argued that the father sought to establish contact, not because he wanted to see the child, but to maintain a level of control over the mother. Domestic violence was therefore part of a constellation of reasons for being concerned about the father's proposals but not, from these mothers' perspectives, the sole or primary one.

Figure 5.2: Satisfaction with the preparation of the welfare report

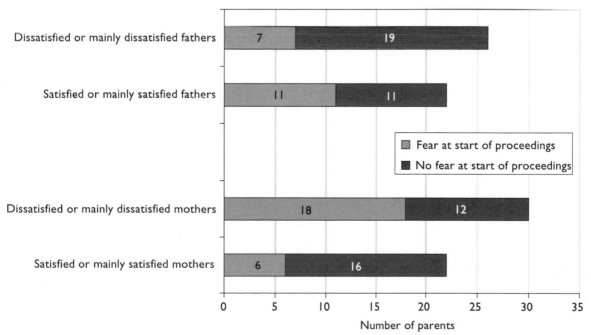

Note: n=100.

A mother who was critical about how domestic violence was addressed by the FCWO

Ms X was dissatisfied with every aspect of the preparation of the welfare report and critical of how the FCWO dealt with issues of domestic violence. There had been incidents of violence while the parents lived together and a further incident on separation. Ms X told the FCWO that she was afraid that her ex-partner would be violent towards her if she met him during the preparation of the report. An interview involving the mother and her ex-partner was nevertheless proposed by the FCWO to which she agreed. She felt that her safety was threatened during the interview at the FCWS office.

She said that she had been assured that at no time would she be left alone. In fact, at the beginning of the meeting, the FCWO went out of the room and she was left on her own with her ex-partner. While they were alone, the father became hostile and threatening.

During the meeting she felt intimidated and unable to put her own point of view across. She felt that her ex-partner was given the opportunity to explain his position when she was expected to remain silent. The meeting ended early when the FCWO stopped it on the grounds that Ms X had lost her temper. An incident occurred when the parents left the FCWS office in which the police became involved.

Ms X was not seen on her own by the FCWO despite her specifically requesting this.

Ms X said that her fears for herself and her daughter were not taken seriously in the welfare report. She was highly critical of the recommendation that direct contact should commence, as she believed this threatened her safety and that of her daughter.

A mother who was complimentary about how domestic violence was addressed by the FCWO

Ms Y had been the victim of persistent abuse throughout her marriage. The father physically assaulted her causing bruising, and would not allow her to leave the house or use the telephone. After leaving the relationship she spent 18 months in a women's refuge. At the time of the interview her address was not to be disclosed to the father.

The father had also physically abused the daughter (a girl aged five at the time of the interview) and there were concerns about sexual abuse. The daughter had been on the social services child protection register.

Ms Y described the FCWO as 'brilliant'. She was offered an appointment at which her ex-partner would be present but also told she could see the FCWO on her own; she chose the latter.

She was satisfied with the arrangements made to assess her daughter's relationship with her father at the FCWS office, both in terms of her own safety and that of her daughter. She wanted contact to be re-established for her daughter but in a way that would ensure their safety. She therefore accepted the recommendation in the welfare report that a gradual build up of contact should take place, starting with supervised contact at a contact centre and moving to contact outside the centre but with handovers taking place at the centre. The order broadly reflected the recommendation. At the time of the interview she said that everyone had benefited from the resumption of contact in a way which focused on safety.

Some of the mothers for whom violence was a current issue recognised that their children loved their fathers and wanted to see them. This was a particularly painful dilemma for them. One mother spent time in a refuge following prolonged and serious violence. Contact was set up in a contact centre despite her fears for herself and her belief that the father would prove unreliable. Nevertheless, she said, "No matter what I have given [child], he still loves his dad. He worships his dad".

It was puzzling that these findings were not entirely consistent with other studies (Hester and Radford, 1996; Radford et al, 1999). The expectation of the researchers had been that a substantial number of mothers in this high-conflict sample would believe that their safety and that of their children had been jeopardised by the court process and contact with the father. The questionnaire had been explicitly designed to allow mothers to express these concerns. The fact that many did not express concerns, however, should not be taken to invalidate other research. The main reason is likely to be that the samples were chosen in different ways.

Concerns about the ex-partner's ability to care for their children

There was a tendency for parents' overall satisfaction with the way the report was prepared to be associated with concerns about the other parent's care of the children. The belief that the FCWO had discounted their worries about the care of their children was often the main reason a parent was dissatisfied with how the report had been prepared.

Expectations and outcomes

Although parents' experiences of the welfare enquiry ranged from very positive to extremely negative, none of the factors so far considered (gender, race, domestic violence or childcare) fully explains why some parents are satisfied and others not. Two other factors, however, do appear to be closely linked with levels of satisfaction. These are attitude to the ordering of the report, which is inversely related to satisfaction, and reaction to the outcome, which is positively linked.

Parents who were critical of how their concerns about the other parent's ability to care for the children were addressed by the FCWO

"If he genuinely loved the children I would not worry about contact, but whenever the children go to him they come back starving and dirty. [Child] has to have gromits, so he can't go swimming – I am petrified that he will take them swimming. If I gave him a letter saying don't take them swimming he would do it. I gave him medicines for weekend contact and he never gave them the medicines. He [child] came back with blood coming out of his mouth, he'd got worse. And whenever I stress this to the judges, my solicitor, the CWO, they say, 'Well he is the father, I'm sure he looks after them as best he can'. Well no. I always have to pick up the pieces after a contact. I am bringing up the kids on my own and I shouldn't have to do that." (Mother)

"The welfare officer didn't seem to want to look into my side of the things that I was saying. It was, 'Well, she's looking after the children and she's the main person that is looking after them'. But she's not doing it, her mum is; but she just didn't seem to see that. She said well she can arrange a babysitter and do what she wants. But what they didn't understand was that her mum works full time and her dad had to be up at five in the morning and she took him to work. The kids have come up smelling ... if the children have stayed down the house with her, they've obviously wet the bed and [child] was coming up smelling of wee and I was having to give them a bath. And her mum and dad had six dogs in a small house." (Father)

"Some of the things she said as soon as I walked through the door ... once we started getting into the conversation and I started to say what had been going on she [FCWO] said, well, basically, 'She's got the children, she's their mother, she can do what she wants'. She didn't say it in those kind of terms but that's how it came across. And I thought, 'What am I doing here, and what is the point of me doing this?' Obviously she wasn't going to look into it and see what was going on." (Father)

Figure 5.3: Parents' attitudes to the welfare report

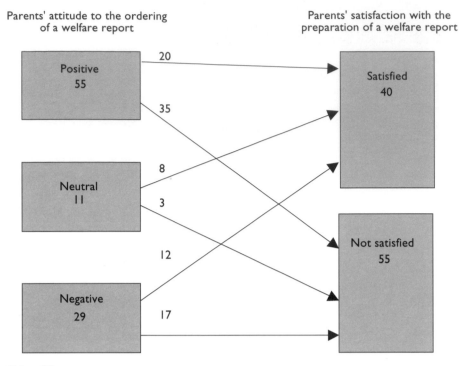

Note: *n*=95.

Figure 5.3 demonstrates the fluidity in parents' attitudes. Two thirds of the parents who were positive about the welfare report being ordered were not satisfied with how it was prepared. Conversely, 40% of those who were negative when the report was ordered were positive about how it was prepared.

Why did parents change their views? At the outset (see Chapter 4) they may have misunderstood the role of the FCWO. Some may have had unrealistic expectations about what could be achieved through the court process; others unjustifiable fears about what would happen. Given that, in general, parents' objectives were incompatible, it was highly probable that one would be disappointed. Some parents appeared to have hoped that the court proceedings would repair fractured relationships or change their ex-partner's behaviour or attitudes. These hopes were almost inevitably dashed. Parents who feared that their children would be taken from them or that they were likely to be sent to prison were relieved to discover that these risks were minimal.

"I wanted to be able to see the children, and for them to know that I loved them and hadn't just walked away. I was prepared to move heaven and earth to see them." (Father)

"I hoped that their father would come to his senses and would not use contact to get at me." (Mother)

"I was afraid of being put in prison. The solicitor said that mothers who didn't agree to contact would be put in prison and that the children would be forced to see their father." (Mother)

The only strong predictor of satisfaction with the preparation of the welfare report is reaction to outcome (see Figure 5.4).

Parents who did not achieve what they had hoped were critical of the way the report was prepared. On the other hand, most parents who were happy with the outcome were pleased with the way it was prepared. Parents had very strong feelings about a decision that affected their relationship with their child, and they believed that the FCWO was highly influential in determining the outcome. It was therefore not surprising that their evaluation of the process reflected what they felt about the outcome.

Figure 5.4: Reaction to outcome and satisfaction with how the welfare report was prepared

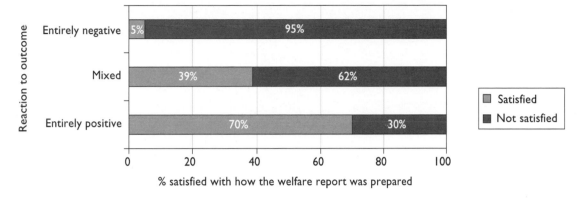

Note: n=95.

The association of outcome and satisfaction does not invalidate the experiences of the parents. Indeed, there were 12 parents who were satisfied with the outcome but critical of the way in which the welfare report was prepared. It does, however, raise questions about how far it would be possible for changes in practice to increase levels of satisfaction for those parents who are currently unhappy with the process.

The family courts and FCWOs stress that their objective is to find an arrangement that is in the best interests of the child, and not to create winners or losers among the parents. Did the parents see the proceedings in this light? In the 27 cases where both parents were interviewed, half the parents had different views on the outcome. Whether these parents saw themselves as 'winners' or 'losers' is not known; it is clear, however, that a satisfactory outcome for one parent was viewed as unsatisfactory by the other (see Table 5.3). In three quarters of these cases parents expressed different levels of satisfaction with the way in which the welfare report was prepared. Again, what was a satisfactory process for one parent was often unsatisfactory for the other.

Table 5.3: Cases where both parents were interviewed (%)

Satisfaction with how the welfare report was prepared	
Mother satisfied/father dissatisfied	37
Father satisfied/mother dissatisfied	41
Both parents satisfied	11
Both parents dissatisfied	11
Reaction to outcome	
Mother more positive than father	33
Father more positive than mother	22
Both parents positive	19
Both parents with mixed feelings	22
Both parents negative	4

Note: n=27.

Have parents' experiences changed?

Over 20 years ago Murch reported that 12% of the parents he interviewed had been dissatisfied with the court welfare officer (Murch, 1980). Some 15 years ago, when Clulow and Vincent (1987) conducted their research as part of a team of FCWOs, they found that "the ratio of complaint to appreciation was in the region of two to one" (p 163). Just over half the parents in this study were either dissatisfied or mainly dissatisfied, and many parents who *were* satisfied with the process nevertheless found it painful and distressing. It is not clear why so many more parents were satisfied in Murch's study, but it would appear that, in the 15 years since the Clulow and Vincent study, a substantial proportion of parents are still dissatisfied with the way in which the welfare report is prepared.

The sledgehammer and the nut

When parents are in dispute about the arrangements for their children, it is highly likely that at least one of them will feel unhappy about how the dispute is handled. Parental separation in itself leads to conflict and mistrust between the parents. The differences that led to the separation are likely to include different ideas about how children should be looked after and brought up. Each parent will have their own view about what is 'in the best interests of their child'. The decision to apply to the court will usually be taken by one parent with the other a reluctant participant. The applicant may be looking for 'justice' from the court and for their rights as a parent to be upheld; instead, they find that the court regards the welfare of the child as paramount (1989 Children Act, Section 1(3)). However, the parent may take a very different view from the court of what is best for their child, and the court's view may, in any case, be difficult to predict. Entry to the court arena will produce uncertainty and a sense of alienation as personal histories are translated into legal discourse.

If parents engaged in legal proceedings about their children want, at some level, to improve a failing relationship or assert a standard of care, they are almost bound to be disappointed by court intervention. The court can only make orders about the time a child spends with a particular person; it cannot order a repaired relationship or a particular family lifestyle. The hands of the FCWO are also tied. The only room for manoeuvre is that given by the parents' willingness to compromise or re-evaluate.

Summary

- 56% of parents were dissatisfied or mainly dissatisfied with the process of welfare reporting. The parents' gender, ethnicity and experience of domestic violence did not go far to explain their different experiences. The main predictors of satisfaction were expectations at the outset (an inverse relationship) and reaction to outcome (positively related).
- Both mothers and fathers (primarily those who were dissatisfied with the process) were critical of a system which each saw as favouring the parent of the opposite sex and ignoring their own perspectives and needs.
- Black parents' accounts of the FCWO's sensitivity to issues of ethnicity, culture and religion were mixed; 20% believed that their race, culture or religion had counted against them.
- Seven out of eleven mothers for whom domestic violence was an issue in the proceedings were dissatisfied with the process. However, violence was not, in their view, the key factor in making a decision about the arrangements for their child.
- Many parents believed that their concerns about how the other parent looked after their child were discounted by the FCWO.

Outcomes one year on

Family Law is inherently unenforceable in the traditional sense since it attempts to regulate intimate human relationships. Parents cannot ultimately be forced to see children, or children to see parents. (Bainham, 1998a, p 2)

Since this was the first study to examine outcomes for children who had been subject to a welfare report, the researchers had little idea what they would find when they reinterviewed parents 12 months on. How many arrangements would still be in place? Would there be any difference between cases that were adjudicated and those that were agreed outside court? Would there still be high levels of conflict? Would parents and children be displaying lower levels of stress?

Not unexpectedly, it did not prove possible to follow up all the original interviewees. Although all the parents had agreed to be contacted again, experience suggested that a degree of sample attrition was to be expected. In the event, 81 parents in 62 cases were reinterviewed: just over 80%. Both parents were reinterviewed in 19 cases, compared to the original sample of 27 'couples'.

Analysis of the cases and parents who had been 'lost' to the research indicated that the spread was fairly even across the sample. In terms of reported satisfaction with outcome there was a slight preponderance of parents with more negative views but the differences were small. Unfortunately, it was only possible to reinterview in two thirds of cases involving black families, 'perpetual litigants' and cases going to the High Court.

Did the arrangements made in the court proceedings persist?

Residence arrangements were remarkably stable, the only change being one young man who had first opted to move to live with his father and then had moved out to live with his grandfather.

Contact was much more changeable (Figure 6.1). There were only 24 (of 59) cases in which the contact arrangements were the same as those set up in the court proceedings. Further, in ten of these the arrangements had either been seriously disrupted or one parent had tried to make changes.

> **Example: Two children aged 8 and 5, agreed contact order, alternate weekends staying contact**
> Staying contact continued as per the order for three months, then stopped. The parents disagreed on why this had happened. Contact was re-established, but the father reported serious problems in managing the behaviour of the older child. The mother refused to agree to separate contact for each child so contact again stopped. The child with behaviour problems was referred to a therapist, who also saw both parents. The mother agreed to re-establish contact, with children initially going separately to their father. At the time of the second interview staying contact as originally arranged had just restarted.

However, it is important to note that, in half the cases in which arrangements at the second interview were different, this was because the amount or level of contact had increased (for example, from visiting to staying contact) and/or the arrangements had

Figure 6.1: Persistence of contact arrangements

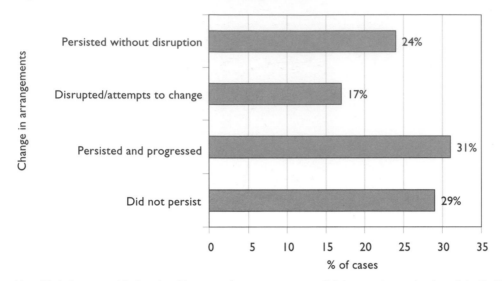

Note: *Excludes cases with shared residence or where parents were still living together at the time of the final hearing. *n*=59. Percentages added to more than 100% because of rounding up.

Figure 6.2: Stability of contact arrangements by nature of contact ordered

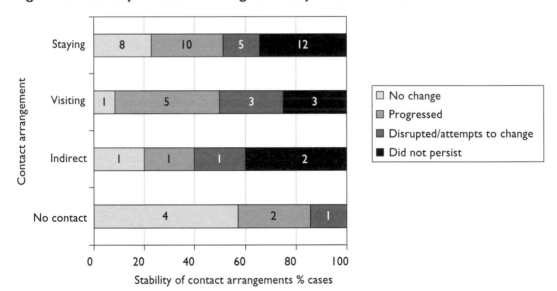

Note: n=59.

become more flexible. In one such case there was no doubt that the changes were benign and on the whole welcomed by both parents.

"We've generally stuck to what was agreed but the arrangements have become more relaxed – if something comes up we can swap. It's usually in favour of them [the father and new partner], but there's no point in forcing the issue if [child] wants to do it and we haven't got anything planned." (Mother)

"Things are more flexible, for example, sometimes [child] will come on Sunday morning, if we're going out in the afternoon, [child] might come out with us. That's about 100% improvement on what we had in the past." (Father)

In contrast in the remaining half, either the amount of contact had reduced, or contact had moved down a level and in eight cases contact had ceased.

As one might expect, arrangements providing for *no contact* were the most stable (Figure 6.2). Even so there were two 'no contact' cases in which contact was now taking place, and one in which a parent was still trying to make indirect contact.

Arrangements for *visiting contact* were the least stable, persisting without disruption or attempts to change in only one of the twelve cases. In a quarter of cases the arrangements were subject to disruption or unsuccessful attempts at change, and in another quarter either the level or the amount of contact diminished. On the other hand, these cases were the ones most likely to change in the direction of increased levels or amounts of contact and/or greater flexibility.

Did the mode of dispute resolution make any difference?

Overall the mode of dispute resolution made little difference to the stability of the contact arrangements. Omitting cases in which no direct contact was ordered (since these have the least scope for change) and focusing on those in which the original dispute was about contact reveals some interesting differences (Figure 6.3).

Thus, cases settled prior to the day of the court hearing were the most likely to progress to more contact; those going to a contested hearing most likely to persist unchanged; and those settling at the

door of the court most likely to fail. Taken together, these figures would appear to lend some weight to the intuitive belief that parents who are able to reach agreement in the course of proceedings are more likely to be able to negotiate changes in the future than those who maintain their dispute to the door of the court and beyond, and that agreements reached on the day carry a greater risk of breaking down.

Parental satisfaction with arrangements at time of second interview

Three in five interviewees said that they were either completely or mainly satisfied with the arrangements in place at the time of the follow-up interview. The rest were almost evenly split between those who were mainly dissatisfied and those who were entirely dissatisfied (Figure 6.4).

Relationship between levels of parental satisfaction and the stability of the contact

Responses to assess how the levels of parental satisfaction related to the stability or otherwise of the contact established by the court proceedings were obtained from 77 parents. The highest levels of satisfaction were expressed by parents who were either persisting with the original contact arrangements unchanged or had different arrangements involving an increase in contact (Figure

Figure 6.3: Stability of contact arrangements by nature of dispute resolution

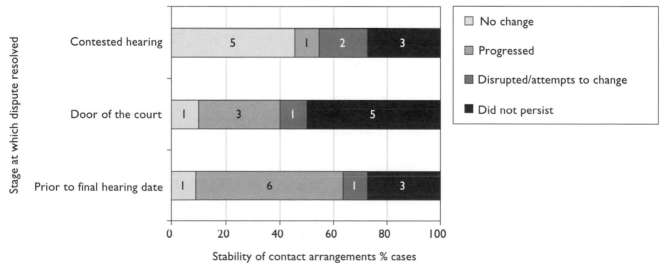

Note: *n*=32.

6.5). Surprisingly, however, the satisfaction levels expressed by parents in cases where the arrangements had neither persisted nor progressed were only slightly lower. The only group in which a majority of parents were dissatisfied were those where the contact arrangements were still essentially the same but had either been substantially disrupted at some point or at least one parent had tried, unsuccessfully, to get them altered. Such parents also tended to be extremely discontented, over a third saying they were entirely dissatisfied. Similarly, although there were only eight dissatisfied parents in cases where arrangements had neither persisted nor progressed, all

but one of them said they were entirely dissatisfied. Discontented parents in the other two groups were more likely to label themselves as mainly dissatisfied.

As Figure 6.6 indicates, there was some consistency in parental levels of satisfaction at the two interview points. Nonetheless, there has evidently been some shifting of views.

Most of the parents who were originally entirely positive were less satisfied 12 months on. Only 11 were still entirely satisfied, with 11 mainly satisfied, three mainly dissatisfied and six entirely dissatisfied.

Figure 6.4: Overall levels of satisfaction

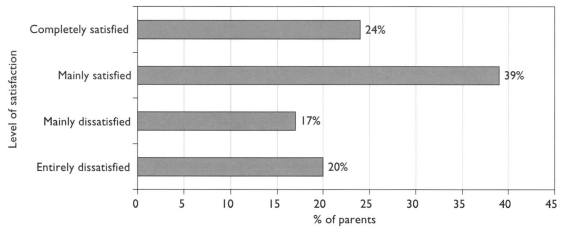

Note: One parent felt unable to express an opinion because arrangements had changed so recently.
n=80.

Figure 6.5: Parental satisfaction with current arrangements by whether arrangements persisted

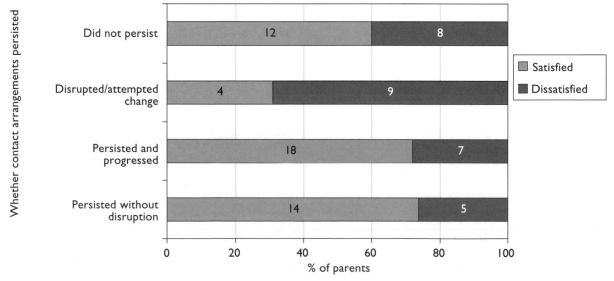

Note: n=77.

Figure 6.6: Parental satisfaction post-proceedings by views at second interview

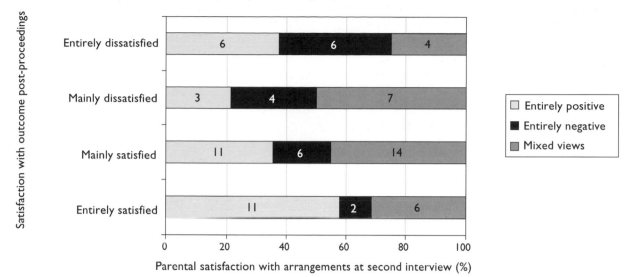

Note: n=70.

Of the 31 who had originally held mixed views, opinions had become marginally more positive with six now being entirely satisfied and only four entirely dissatisfied. Similarly only a minority (6) of the parents (18) who were originally entirely negative remained entirely dissatisfied.

What explains the shifting positions?

In general these shifts of opinion can be explained by developments post-proceedings.

• Where arrangements had *progressed* all nine initially positive parents expressed themselves either completely or mainly satisfied with developments. Conversely, of the seven parents who had been entirely negative in the first instance, two were mainly satisfied a year later.
• Where arrangements had been *disrupted* or where there had been *unsuccessful attempts to change* both groups of parents were largely dissatisfied. However, while the originally positive parents had become less satisfied, there was a shift towards a less negative view among the four parents who had been originally completely negative.
• Where arrangements had *not persisted* the shifts of opinion were most marked, as one might expect given that the new arrangements might be more or less favourable to the person being interviewed.

Five of the ten parents who had been positive about the original arrangements said they were wholly or largely dissatisfied with the changes. Conversely, both of the initially dissatisfied parents were now wholly satisfied.
• It is interesting to note, however, that where arrangements *persisted unchanged*, three of the originally entirely positive parents were now only mainly satisfied, while three of the four who had been entirely negative were now only mainly dissatisfied, or even mainly satisfied.

The involvement of the court

Only a third of cases in which the contact arrangements changed had been back to court. Moreover, it was noticeable that, whereas most increases in contact did involve court action, there had been proceedings in only five of the 17 cases in which contact was reduced. Where there had been court proceedings, these were more likely to involve a new action or an unanticipated review.

Around 35% of the cases had been back to court, but around half of these were because of a review previously ordered by the court. There were only eight cases in which there were either fresh proceedings or an unanticipated review. All but two of these new actions were initiated by non-resident fathers; three to enforce contact orders, one to change residence and two to deal with details of

Figure 6.7: Parental relationship at second interview

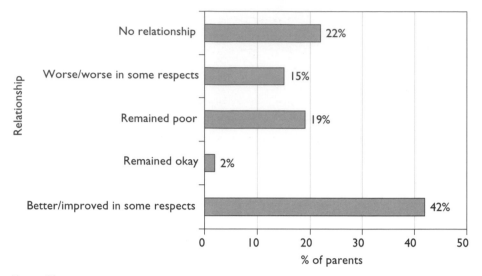

Note: n=81.

contact. The exceptions were applications by resident parents (one father, one mother) to reduce contact. Ominously, however, in a further 19% of cases, at least one parent told us that they were considering going back to court.

Parental relationships

Parental relationships at the time proceedings were instigated were, as reported in Chapter 2, generally dire. A year or so after proceedings had ended, about a fifth said they did not have a relationship while a third reported relationships which had remained poor or had deteriorated further, either overall, or in some respects (Figure 6.7).

To counter this depressing picture, a third of parents reported that their relationship was better, while a further tenth indicated some improvement. However, as can be seen from the following examples, it was, at most, a fairly uneasy rapprochement.

"It was initially a lot better – after the proceedings things were amicable. We even went to visit secondary schools together, had discussions about which one was best. But it's deteriorated over the last few months. I've tried so hard, but I get shot down. Last time we spoke we had a blazing row over the 'phone; I had to be restrained by my partner from going up to his house; they would have had to call the police." (Resident mother)

"I don't see how we're going to move forward. I can't see an end to the conflict." (Resident mother)

"We're not friends – it's easier than it was, but it's only polite. There is no real relationship. We put the best side forward for [child]. Basically he won; I felt once it was settled there was no point fighting." (Resident mother)

"It has got better - things are a lot more amicable. Last week I even had an impromptu game of cricket with him and [elder child]. That was nice. There's been no repetition of the harassment. We have occasional rows; things can still get fiery." (Resident mother)

Men and women were equally likely to report improved or deteriorated relationships. Indeed, in the 19 'couple' cases there was a remarkable congruence of opinion about the current state of play.

Conflict and domestic violence

Given the high levels of conflict and hostility reported earlier, these were dimensions of the parental relationship which the research was specifically concerned to explore. Of the 66 parents who considered that they still had a relationship, of sorts, just under a half said that levels of conflict were either just as bad or had got worse. However, just over a half reported improvement.

Of the 40 mothers who had reported themselves victims of domestic violence, 32 were reinterviewed. Of these, five said that they had been frightened of the other parent during the last year.

Example

One of these was a mother whose current concern was not so much violence to herself but the safety of the children. After repeated court proceedings she had finally managed to get an order for contact in a tightly supervised contact centre. She was understandably terrified when her ex-partner "chased me across the fields" as she left the centre, although mercifully, as it transpired, nothing untoward occurred. This mother was one of two parents who considered that the contact arrangements had exposed them to the risk of violence.

Two other mothers reported specific incidents in which there had been perceived intimidation or threats, and one mother described an assault. None of the fathers reinterviewed reported violence or fear, although there were some accounts of high conflict encounters on the doorstep.

"There was an angry 'phone call between us, he came round to the flat, pushed me to the ground and ran upstairs. He fought with my partner on the stairs. My partner put a headlock on him. Then we all went inside and talked calmly. His power had been effectively challenged." (Mother)

"She and her sister were firing abuse at me, they said I had hit [mother]. I was afraid she would chuck something. She was shouting in front of [the child] who was crying, and saying, 'Mummy, no, no'." (Father)

The children

Child welfare and safety concerns

At first interview almost two thirds of parents expressed concerns about the parenting behaviour or capacity of their ex-partner, as described in Chapter 2. A year later this was still a common theme, although the proportion had dropped to a half of parents in cases where there was still contact. Again, concerns mainly centred on what might be termed lax or inattentive parenting, particularly in relation to boundary setting and standards of behaviour, education and healthcare. While these could be interpreted simply as differences in approach (which, as some parents recognised, they and the children just had to accommodate), it is nevertheless important to emphasise that they reflected genuinely-held worries about the care that children were receiving while with the other parent, and its effect on their long-term well being.

"I have general concerns. It's his way of life – it's more lax – he lets her sip alcohol, smoke cigarettes. He gives her more freedom than I would, for example with boys. The influence from school is there all the time and now there's the influence of another family with different standards. Children just follow who they mix with. I feel my influence is diminished." (Resident mother of child aged 11)

"There's no balance in his life – it is all fun and games. I have no influence, for example, my son wanted to have body piercing I said no, but his father got it done anyway. He also allowed him to have his head shaved. [The child] is dyslexic and the school isn't very good, but his father isn't interested." (Non-resident mother of child aged 11)

Cases in which either parent expressed specific fears about the child's safety or which involved allegations of abuse, were less usual, although there were two cases of alleged sexual abuse and four of possible physical abuse. Three parents also considered their children to be subject to emotional abuse. There were four cases in which social services had become involved, and one had led to a child protection investigation.

Parents' views on what their children thought

A total of 56 parents considered their children to be either completely or mainly happy with the arrangements in place by second interview. If we exclude the 14 who felt unable to answer (typically because they were not in direct contact), this amounts to 84% of parents. As might be expected, there was a strong correlation between parental satisfaction with the current arrangements and their perceptions of the children's views.

While some might interpret this cynically as meaning that parents see children through the lens of their own needs, one could equally conclude that these parents had managed to ensure that the arrangements did accord with what the children wanted. There is some support for this in the fact that 13 parents (five fathers and eight mothers) reported that their children were happy with the arrangements even though they themselves were not. It was more unusual for a parent to say that they were satisfied, although they were aware that the children were not (two mothers, one father).

Only 30 children were interviewed, and these children had a rather different perspective (as will be seen in Chapter 7) and possibly one that was not easy to share with their parent(s). Only half said they had got what they wanted. This response appeared to be different from their answer to the more emotional question, 'Were you happy with the decision?', to which only a third responded positively.

Children's exposure to conflict and hostility

"If there is any stress between us [at handovers] she will disappear. If we're chatting she will glow."
(Mother)

As described earlier, a year after proceedings had ended there had been some abatement in levels of conflict and hostility. However, the proportion of cases in which at least one parent said the children were still aware of tensions between their parents was worryingly high at 41 (66%).

In keeping with the parents' report, two thirds of interviewed children reported seeing their parents arguing or disagreeing (see Chapter 7); more than a third of the children had seen their parents 'pushing or shoving' in an argument. Around two thirds said that they were made to feel guilty by either their mother or father for wanting to see the other parent. However, how much of this related to their current situation was less clear. Poignantly, just over a quarter of the children said that if it would mean the end to arguments, they would rather not see the other parent.

As will be seen in Chapter 8, the children's ongoing distress was reflected in both the emotional and behavioural scores recorded by their parents and those recorded by themselves.

Summary

- At the second stage all but one of the residence arrangements were stable. In a third of cases contact arrangements progressed to more contact with the non-residential parent, in a quarter they remained unchanged. In just under half the cases the level of contact was reduced or there had been serious disruption to the arrangements.
- Cases which were settled without a court hearing were more likely to progress to more, or more flexible contact, and the parents were more likely to be satisfied with the outcome at the second stage.
- Half the mothers for whom domestic violence had been an issue during the proceedings said they had been frightened of the other parent during the year between the two interviews. Two mothers believed that the contact arrangements had exposed them to the risk of violence.
- Most parents believed that their children were happy with the arrangements a year on but, as will be seen in Chapter 7, only a third of the children described themselves as happy with the decision.
- A year after proceedings had ended there was some abatement in the levels of conflict and hostility, but in two thirds of cases parents reported that their children were still aware of the tensions between them and the other parent.

7

Children's voices

While a great deal is known about the effects of divorce on children, less is known about how far children are actively involved during the divorce process and to what extent if at all they have any say in what actually happens to them post-divorce. (Scanlan et al, 2001, p 34)

To date, none of the growing body of research into children's views of the divorce process has focused specifically on children who are the subject of welfare reports. In Douglas et al's (2000) study of a representative sample of recently divorced families, only five of the children were the subject of proceedings for Section 8 orders under the 1989 Children Act.

This chapter centres on the subsample of 30 children who were interviewed. Although, as we saw in Chapter 2, these 30 children were well matched to the total sample of 116 children who were the subject of proceedings, with such a small sample, caution needs to be exercised in interpreting the findings. Because of the tentative nature of the findings, the full breakdown of the figures is presented so that the reader can draw their own conclusions from the data. The children's quotations are necessarily quite stark, as it was felt that giving more information may have lead to some children being identified.

The children's experiences of their parents' separation

Parental separation constituted a crisis in the children's lives, characterised by an acute sense of shock, disbelief and emotional distress.... To some extent the impact of parental separation on the children was directly related to whether and how information about the separation and its consequences were communicated. Few children were adequately prepared by their parents. (Douglas et al, in press)

Some of the children interviewed in this study reflected the findings from the Douglas et al study, but for other children, their parental separation and divorce was less well remembered. A difference in this study is that, although the majority of children reported that their parents had lived together (27 out of 30), not all the children's parents had been married. In the Douglas et al study all the parents had been married.

Only half of the children in this study knew why their parents had split up. In the Douglas et al study, although 99% of parents reported that they had told their children about the divorce, only 71% of the children recalled being told. Overall, as in the Douglas et al study, most children felt poorly informed about what had happened in their lives.

In planning the children's interviews eleven children took part in the focus groups at contact centres. These children gave a clearer picture. They fell into three groups: those who *knew the reason* for their parents separating; those who were *aware of the rowing*; and those for whom the parental separation came as *a complete surprise*. Those who felt they knew the reasons for the separation or had been aware of the arguments considered that they were better able to come to terms with it than those for whom it had been a complete surprise.

How did you find out about your mum and dad's separation?

"I can't remember – I was little. I found out a few years ago. I thought dad was on holiday."

"Mum actually told me she wanted a word with me and I went upstairs. She said she was leaving and going to live elsewhere."

"It's easier to cope with when you know why they are separating." (Young person at contact centre)

"On that particular day my dad picked us up from school and said, 'Right, I am leaving you', and I said, 'No you are not', and he said, "Yes I am, it's true', and then we got home ... and he left and I cried."

What difference did it make for you?

Those children who had some memory of their parents' separation were then asked what difference they felt it would make to their lives at the time. Seven children said they thought it would make some or a lot of difference, while another seven thought it might not make much difference. The remainder did not know or chose not to say. Ten children reckoned that, overall, things had actually worked out for the better, but another 12 had a mixed or negative reaction. Five children specifically mentioned a reduction in arguing as a reason why it was better and two children mentioned positive relationships with stepparents. Throughout the study, a key determinant for the children of things getting better was a reduction in the arguing and conflict.

When your parents separated did they ask you whom you wanted to live with?

Whereas in the Douglas study 45% of the children at the time of the parental separation had been asked whom they wanted to live with, only nine children in this study said they had been consulted. More than half, however, had been asked how often and when

they would like to see the parent who was no longer living with them.

How has it worked out for you?

"I think it is better like this, 'cos I see them just the same, and they are not arguing when you go and see them and you can do more things."

"It is just below 'for the better'. It is not as good as them living together."

"I'm not sure, I am glad, but quite a lot of the time I want them to be together. But then I am glad because I feel really close to my stepparents."

"Well obviously I miss them, the cats; I miss the talks we have together."

"I live with both of them. There are seven days in the week, so I would stay with my dad for four days and my mum three days. I wish there were even days in the week."

The experience of the welfare reporting

As in the Douglas et al study, children had little knowledge and understanding of the legal processes, but those who remember seeing the FCWO were often quite clear about their role.

Around two thirds of the children knew why they were the seeing the FCWO and thought that seeing a FCWO would be useful. Seven children felt that they had no choice about seeing the FCWO. Many children had anxieties about it.

Often the children remembered seeing the FCWO a greater or fewer number of times than the number reported by the parents, or stated in the court welfare report. This reflects children's unclear memories of the sequence of events and the role of professionals that they saw at the time (for example, there was some confusion between FCWOs and solicitors or therapists). Seven out of ten children said they liked the FCWO. The attribute described most often about FCWOs was that they were 'friendly'. Very few children felt that there was anything they did not like about the FCWO.

What does the FCWO do?

"The FCWO sees the children and asks them what they want, they listen to the adults as well, and ask what they want, they write a report on what they think everybody wants, and everybody else reads it."

"They make a statement of what mum said and what dad said, and the sort of environment that both parents live in and they give the judge or whatever their own opinion, I think."

What did you think of having to see the FCWO?

"I didn't really know who I wanted to live with, and I didn't really want to choose either."

"Might help life being a bit better seeing mum and dad at the same time; it is hard."

What were the things you liked about the FCWO?

"She was not on anyone's side; she was not telling me what to do."

"She was just normal, you know what I mean? She wasn't very forceful; she didn't intimidate me or anything. Just a normal person."

"She was kind, she talked to you like she knew about it, like she had been there."

"She was understanding, she explained most things in a way that I could understand."

Was there anything you did not like about the FCWO?

"[FCWO] did not tell me there was going to be a report. [FCWO] treated me as if I am younger than I am."

"She kept changing your words, messing your head. Changed your words to things that were not true. I wanted to see her on my own – she should have interviewed me separately first, then with my parents. You can't say what you want in front of your sister or parent."

Table 7.1: Seeing the FCWO

	Good	Mixed	Bad	NA	Don't know	Missing
What did you think of the FCWO?	15	5	0	3	6	1

	Yes	Mixed	No	NA	Don't know	Missing
Did you like the FCWO?	21	1	0	3	5	0

	Yes	Perhaps	No	NA	Don't know	Missing
Did the FCWO explain what they were there for?	18	1	3	4	3	1
Did the FCWO listen to you?	23	0	1	3	2	1
Do you think the FCWO understood what you felt/wanted?	11	1	2	1	3	12
Do you think the FCWO took what you were saying seriously?	21	1	1	4	3	0
Were you worried that the FCWO might tell your mum/dad/judge what you were telling them?	5	3	17	3	2	0
Did you want the FCWO to tell your mum/dad/judge what you were saying?	10	1	10	1	5	3
Was there anything you wanted to say but did not feel able to?	5	1	17	3	3	1

The majority of children thought that the FCWO explained what they were there for and listened seriously to them. When it came to the question 'Do you think the FCWO understood what you felt/ wanted?', half the children chose not to reply to this question or felt unable to answer, while another three children said 'perhaps' or 'no'. It is possible that some of the non-responses were also implying a negative reply. More than a quarter of the children worried about the FCWO telling their parents or the judge what they had said, but another third of the children wanted this to happen. A central concern for many of the children was that in saying what they wanted there might be possible repercussions from the other parent. Children, after many years of parental conflict, become experts in diplomacy. Five children said that there were things they had wanted to say to the FCWO but did not feel able to. A few children felt restricted in what they could say because another member of their family was in the room at the time.

Only three children mentioned that the FCWO had asked their school about them. All other children thought that just family members had been involved in the process. This is interesting, as the school had been asked to provide information on the child and their family in most cases (see Chapter 5).

About half the children talked to their parents afterwards about what happened and knew what was decided. Only half said the result was what they wanted and only a third felt happy about the decision. Half the children felt 'mixed' or actively 'unhappy' about what had been decided.

What did you want to say but not feel able to?

"I could say everything when dad wasn't there; otherwise I was embarrassed as there would be a scene."

Were you worried about what the FCWO might say in the report?

"I was very careful about what I said."

"She thought I wanted to live with my mum more; I didn't want her to tell my dad in case his feelings were hurt."

"I wanted the FCWO to tell the judge but not to tell my parents – [FCWO] said it was only between you and me, but [FCWO] told my parents."

What did you feel after you saw the FCWO?

"I felt better, more relieved that I had got certain things out."

"Nothing really changed."

"I felt quite proud that I had told someone how I felt and that it would make a difference."

"I guess I was thinking that I should have felt happy for my mum, and happy for me, and sad for my dad and sad for me."

Table 7.2: After seeing the FCWO

	Yes	Not sure/ sort of	No	NA	Don't know	Missing
Did you talk to your mum/dad about what happened?	16	0	6	4	4	0
Do you know what was decided?	15	3	5	1	4	2
Did you want to know?	16	3	3	1	2	5
Is this what you wanted to happen?	15	4	3	3	2	3
Thinking back, should mum and dad have been allowed to do this [go to court]?	17	3	3	0	3	4
Should children be allowed to go to court themselves?	12	3	7	1	6	1
Do you think there should be someone there just for you (and sibling)?	20	4	2	1	1	2

	Happy	Mixed	Unhappy	NA	Don't know	Missing
How did you feel about the decision?	10	12	3	1	2	2

When asked if they would have liked the FCWO to talk to them afterwards, some children thought that would have been useful, whereas others thought that their parents were able to tell them everything they needed to know.

Children were somewhat unsure as to whether the court process had helped them. Seven children did not know, two children said it did not help, and eight children expressed, with resignation, that it had helped, as a 'last resort'.

Thinking back – did it help that your mum and dad went to court?

"Helped? Not really, it is just the same."

"Well, they weren't going to sort it out any other way, so that was the final resort I think."

"Yes. Although I feel as if I could have actually told my dad in the first place that that was what I wanted, and they might not have had to go to court."

"Yes, it helped because it stopped the arguments."

"Sometimes I really want to go to my dad's and I can't, and sometimes I really want to go to my mum's and I can't. Although I am sure that my mum and dad would let me, it would be against what the court ordered."

Could there have been a better way of sorting out the arrangements?

"If you could talk to family members instead of strangers who don't really know the other people – it could be a friend, informal."

"It was the last resort. They didn't speak or anything. They didn't ring each other up; there was no contact between them."

Nine children had suggestions about how the dispute could have been sorted out earlier without recourse to the courts. However, for 11 children the dispute had become so difficult for them that they thought of the court process as the last resort – the only way of sorting out the arrangements.

Table 7.3: The decision-making process

Who would you like to have been involved? (n=30)			Who was involved (in child's view)? (n=18)	
25	(83%)	Me	8	(44%)
25	(83%)	Mum	13	(72%)
21	(70%)	Dad	12	(67%)
10	(33%)	Sibling	3	(17%)
16	(53%)	Friend	0	
16	(53%)	FCWO	7	(39%)
11	(37%)	Grandmother	0	
10	(33%)	Grandfather	0	
0		Judge	9	(50%)

The decision-making process

There has been considerable discussion about the representation of children (for a summary of recent and ongoing research see O'Quigley, 1999). In this study children were asked who they would have liked to be involved in helping their parents sort out their arrangements, which was then compared with data on who they said had actually been involved (Table 7.3).

Five children answered that they didn't know who had been involved, and for a further seven children, no data was obtained for this question. The main conclusion was that *more children wished to be involved than currently are.* Most children demonstrated that they were acutely aware that the whole process was because of, and about them, and they wished to have a say. Those that did not want to be involved were generally anxious about the repercussions of voicing an opinion, especially in front of a parent who might be upset. An interesting finding was the number of children who would have liked 'a friend', grandmother or grandfather present at the decision making. For some children it was apparent that they may want an 'advocate' outside the immediate family to support them. Others wanted to be part of a team, and recognised that other members of the family would have different opinions from their own.

You have/have not put yourself in the decision-making picture – why is this?

"Because it is me that the decisions are about. I have the right to say what I want."

"When the person asked me the questions ... I didn't want her to ask any questions."

"I didn't know who I wanted to live with, and I didn't really want to choose either ... because I couldn't decide."

"It's about me – I want to see my dad."

"So I have some sort of say, and I want to know what other people think as well."

"I did not want to be involved – it was easier."

"I don't like talking about it – it makes me feel bad."

"I do not want to make decisions with my brother. I want decisions about my life to be made independently."

How would you like to be involved?

"I would not like to have the whole say but have other people's opinions."

"I wouldn't like to be too involved, I'd just like to see what other people think."

"Well, I would like to make my point clear, and then let people say what they think about that, so that they can tell me the good and bad points of what I have suggested."

Children going to court themselves

"Children shouldn't be allowed to go to court because it can be quite stressing on them."

"Ask children questions about their views: sometimes their views are childish, or mature; sometimes the child is very determined to go to court. The most important thing is whether they want to go, the second is whether they are mature enough in their views."

It was also interesting that nearly half the young people (usually the older ones) felt that children should be allowed to go to court themselves if they so wished.

Of all the questions, asking the children whether there should be someone there for them prompted the most positive answers. Two thirds of the children wanted to have someone 'there' to support them.

Living in conflict

We perhaps we need to do more talking with children to find out the best ways of listening to them. (Scanlan et al, 2001)

At the centre of the FWCO's work is identifying effective ways of eliciting the views of children and young people who are living in a situation of parental conflict, and who may be frightened to say what they feel. In this study, children reported that most FCWOs had 'talked' to them. With some of the younger children, the FCWOs had involved them in drawing and sometimes the children had undertaken

Table 7.4: Family support questions

	True	Sort of true	Not true	Don't know/ missing
My parents are happier when I am with them than when I am not	22	2	1	5
It would upset me if other kids asked a lot of questions about my parents	7	8	13	2
I feel that my parents still love me	27	2	0	1
I find it difficult to tell my parents what I really want	7	12	10	1
Sometimes worries about my family get in the way of schoolwork	10	2	17	1
Sometimes I am so worried about my family that I stay awake at night	3	4	22	1
I have lots of good friends to whom I can talk to about my family	23	3	2	2

a 'genogram' or family tree. The children's responses did not indicate that particularly sophisticated methods of communicating with children had been involved. As we have seen, many children were anxious about voicing any opinion, which, in their fraught home life, might spark off another conflict. There may be more fruitful ways of communicating with children to assess their views.

In this study, building on the work of Douglas et al (in press), a one-page 'quiz' was developed for the children. This proved an effective method of eliciting sensitive information in a non-threatening way. Children were asked to tick 'true', 'sort of true' 'not true' or 'dk/na' (don't know/not applicable) to 35 questions. If children did not want to answer the question it was suggested they ticked the 'dk/na' box.

The full questionnaire can be seen in Appendix C. For the purpose of this analysis, different aspects are grouped together. The first group of questions was about their *family and the support they had* - whether, for example, they felt they could talk to their friends about their family problems (see Table 7.4).

The majority (but not all) of the children thought that their parents are happier when they are with them than not, and an even greater number of children thought that their parents still loved them. However, 19 children thought it was difficult to tell their parents what they really wanted (if it was easier to tell them, maybe court could have been avoided). Half the children said that they would be upset if other children asked a lot of questions about their parents and seven children said that they are sometimes so worried about their family that they stay awake at night. For 12 children, worries about their family got in the way of schoolwork (that is, the wider effects of family conflict). However Douglas et

al (2000) have shown that peers are an important source of support, and 26 children said that they had lots of good friends to whom they could talk to about their family, which may have a protective effect.

Relationship with dad

The second area of questions focused on the child's relationship with their father. As we saw in Chapter 1, there is a growing literature showing the protective role of 'involved' fathers. Research is less certain about the beneficial effects of father involvement when contact with fathers is associated with severe conflict between parents. A central factor appears to be the nature of the child's existing relationship with the father.

Around two thirds of the children reported that they got on really well with their dad, had a good time when with him, that they could talk to him whatever worries he had, and that he was interested in how they did at school (see Table 7.5). Only six children mentioned being scared of their dad and four that spending time with him interfered with what they want to do at the weekend.

Relationship with mum

The next set of questions related to the child's relationship with their mother.

Around two thirds of the children reported that they got on really well with their mum, and that they could talk to her whatever worries she had. A slightly higher proportion said that they had a good time when with her, and that she was interested in how

Table 7.5: Relationship with dad

	True	Sort of true	Not true	Don't know/ missing
My dad and I get on really well	17	5	6	2
Whatever worries my dad has, I know it is OK for me to talk to him about things that bother me	12	7	8	3
My dad is interested in how I do at school	21	4	1	4
I usually have a good time when I am with dad	21	3	3	3
I am scared of my dad	2	4	21	3
Spending time with dad interferes with what I want to do at the weekend	3	1	21	5

Table 7.6: Relationship with mum

	True	Sort of true	Not true	Don't know/ missing
My mum and I get on really well	21	5	3	1
Whatever worries my mum has I know it is OK for me to talk to her about things that bother me	21	2	5	2
My mum is interested in how I do at school	25	1	2	2
I usually have a good time when I am with my mum	25	2	2	1
I am scared of my mum	3	2	25	0
Spending time with my mum interferes with what I want to do at the weekend	3	3	19	5

Table 7.7: Levels of conflict between parents

	True	Sort of true	Not true	Don't know/ missing
My mum says critical things about my dad when I am with her	3	9	13	5
My dad says critical things about my mum when I am with him	9	6	10	5
My mum makes me feel guilty for wanting to spend time with my dad	4	0	24	2
My dad makes me feel guilty for wanting to spend time with my mum	3	4	19	4
My parents agree about how much time I can spend with each of them	10	4	8	8
My mum and dad often disagree about when and how long I should visit	10	4	9	7
I never see my parents arguing or disagreeing	2	6	20	2
When my parents have an argument they shout at each other	17	5	4	4
My parents have pushed or shoved each other in an argument	8	3	14	5
If it would mean an end to the arguments I would rather not see the non-resident parent	8	1	13	8
Whatever worries my parents have, it does not interfere with my schoolwork	17	3	7	3
I tell mum/dad when I want to see them and they go along with it	8	8	7	7

they did at school. Five children mentioned being scared of their mum and six that spending time with her interfered with what they wanted to do at the weekend. This was an ongoing dilemma for some children, particularly the teenagers, who found contact visits meant that they could not take part in out-of-school activities.

Levels of conflict

The final group of questions was particularly interesting. It is doubtful that the replies would have been so forthcoming had we asked the children directly.

A total of 12 mothers and 15 fathers were reported as saying critical things about the other parent (see Table 7.7). Smaller numbers were reported as making the child feel guilty about wanting to spend time with

the other parent – four mothers and seven fathers made the child feel guilty.

Children viewed making the contact arrangements as a source of conflict for their parents, with only a third of children reporting that their parents agreed about how much time they could spend with each of them, and almost half the children saying that their parents often disagreed about when and for how long they should visit. Just over half the children said that they told their parents when they wanted to see them and the parents went along with it.

Two thirds of the children reported that they had seen their parents arguing or disagreeing and that they shouted at each other while arguing. Eleven children said that their parents had pushed or shoved each other in an argument possibly implying physical violence. Almost a third of children said that if it

Table 7.8: Contact

	Yes	No	No, happy with current arrangements	Don't know/ missing
Have you received letters?	16	9	–	5
Have you received 'phone calls?	20	7	–	3
Have you received presents?	19	7	–	4
Would you like to see mum/dad [non-resident parent] more than you do at the moment?	5	7	2	16

would mean an end to the arguments they would rather not see the non-resident parent.

The findings from the quiz are interesting, but, if they were further developed, they might also have potential for use by FCWOs in assessing children, as will be discussed in Chapter 10.

Children's experience of contact

Whether or not children had direct contact, the majority had indirect contact with the non-resident parent in the form of letters, telephone calls and presents (see Table 7.8). When asked how they felt about this, only three of the children expressed negative comments, while eight expressed positive feelings.

Five children expressed a wish to see their non-resident parent more than they currently did, with two children saying that they were happy with the arrangements and seven saying that they did not want to see the non-resident parent more often. Of the remaining 16, eight did not know or did not feel able to answer. The underlying feeling appeared to be 'it all depends' on the hassle it might involve.

When the children with direct contact were asked whether they ever worried about seeing their non-resident parent, 13 replied that they were not worried. Eight children expressed concerns, with one child worried about being teased by their non-resident parent, one child being upset about seeing their non-resident parent, one worried about whether contact would go well or not, one worried about arguing and one child worried about their

non-resident parent being lonely. The other children did not expand on their reasons for concern.

As we saw in Chapter 6, parents reported that six out of ten contact arrangements had changed in the last year. As can be seen here, the children are also reporting similar fluidity. Arrangements of more than half of the children who saw their non-resident parent said that arrangements had changed in the last year.

The children were asked why the arrangements had changed in the last year (see Table 7.9). Only 13 children answered this question. Six said that they did not know what made the arrangements change. Three children mentioned that one parent moving had affected the contact arrangements; one child mentioned a parent's work, one child said that they were dropped off later as they were older, another child said that it was their wish that contact was altered, and one child mentioned extracurricular activities.

A total of 16 children answered the question 'If it was up to you what would you really like?' Of these, three children said they would like *shared residence*, two would like *increased contact*, two would like *to alter contact details*, five were happy with the status quo and three did not know. One child stated that the parent would have to change their attitude and behaviour for contact to resume. For most children the underlying agenda appeared to be balancing the wish to see a parent more with the conflict and hassle that might result if they did.

Table 7.9: Changing arrangements

	Yes	No	No contact	Don't know/ missing
Have the arrangements changed in the last year?	13	10	5	2

> **If it was up to you what would you really like?**
>
> "Half the week with dad, half the week with mum."
>
> "I wish there were even days in the week!"
>
> "As I do at the moment, I am happy with the arrangements."
>
> "I would like it to stay as it is [no contact]."

When asked what was the best thing about seeing the non-resident parent, some of the children who were not currently having contact recollected past contact time. Many children gave more than one 'best thing' about contact: 15 children mentioned doing activities, playing, treats and having fun; 3 children specifically mentioned seeing their cousins and 7 children mentioned 'just seeing them' (the non-resident parent) or spending time together.

> **What is the best thing about seeing your non-resident parent?**
>
> "Basically just seeing them."
>
> "Cuddles."
>
> "Playing on the computer."
>
> "We play lots more, takes me to my cousins."

The children were asked what the worst thing was about seeing their non-resident parent and whether there was anything that they really didn't like doing. Three children mentioned household chores and homework; four children said that the worst thing was arguing; three children mentioned problems in the transition from one home to another – either the journey or different rules for different homes; and two children mentioned that the contact time was too short. A few children mentioned doing activities, or seeing relatives as the worst thing.

> **What is the worst thing about seeing your non-resident parent?**
>
> "He shouts at us."
>
> "I wanted more time."
>
> "Probably going back to my mum's again, especially after I have spent a long time at my dad's during the holidays, then I find it quite hard switching from one house to another."

> **Is there anything you really don't like doing with your non-resident parent?**
>
> "Going to bed because I go to bed at different times [in each home]."
>
> "I don't like tidying up my room."

What do you do on contact visits?

Information from the children on what they do when they are on contact visits (see Table 7.10) shows that the experience is not dissimilar from what would be expected in a family home in which parents lived together. Other studies have indicated that non-resident fathers merely 'entertain' their children at weekends (see Lamb, 1999), however, this study supports the findings that given visiting or staying contact at weekends *and* in the school week, the non-resident parent is able to maintain a full parent–child relationship (Kelly, 2000). The only problem for some was that contact took place at weekends and holidays when activities would be different wherever they were. The children were asked what different things they did with the non-resident parent as compared to the resident parent. Again, this question was not applicable to children who have no contact. Of the remaining children, 16 replied that things were different and generally mentioned differences in specific activities. Three children said it was similar and two children said it was different because they had supervised contact.

Table 7.10: What do you do on contact visits?

Do you:	Eat meals?	Go out (eg, swimming pool)?	Stay in and watch TV?	Do school work together?	Do school work alone?	Play together?	Play alone?	Visit friends and relatives?
Yes	19	18	17	12	9	18	9	16
No	2	3	4	8	10	2	8	5
NA	8	8	8	8	8	8	8	8
Missing data	1	1	2	2	27	3	5	1

Do you do different things with your non-resident parent than you do at home?

"It's quite similar I think."

"We went ice-skating with my mum and bowling with my dad."

What activities at home/school do you miss when you are with your non-resident parent?

"I don't miss out – he takes us there."

"I miss my cats and my mum, and the other animals, and my friend."

"I miss playing with the cat. I miss the cat, that's it really."

"I don't watch TV; he doesn't like me going on the computer."

As mentioned in Chapter 3, parents are sometimes in conflict over the children's activities and how to fit these in with contact with the non-resident parent as well as spending adequate time with the resident parent. The children were asked what activities at home or school they missed when they were with the non-resident parent. Six children said that they did not miss anything, four children mentioned their pets, two children mentioned the other parent and three their friends. Four children said that they sometimes missed one of their activities and three children said they missed watching TV (perhaps those children who were out doing activities with their non-resident parent).

Memories

Of the children who are not having contact with their non-resident parent, only one child was not sure if they had any memories of their parent (see Table 7.11). Of the eight children who had memories, no children recalled positive memories: four recalled negative memories and four mixed memories. The children were asked if they would like to know more about their non-resident parent: six children answered that they would not like to know more, the remaining children did not answer.

Table 7.11: Memories of parent no longer seen

	Yes	No	Don't know	NA
Do you have any memories of your non-resident parent?	8	0	1	21

	Negative	Mixed		NA
If yes, are they good or bad?	4	4		22

	Yes	No	Don't know	NA
Do you see any of your non-resident parent's family?	17	13		
Would you like to see more of your non-resident parent's family?	8	10	6	6

Over half of the 30 children saw other members of their non-resident parent's family. The children mentioned grandparents, aunts and uncles; six children said they had brothers or sisters who were living elsewhere including elder and younger half- and stepsiblings. Ten children said they were happy with the amount of time they spent with their non-resident parent's family, and six children said that they did not know if they would like to see their family more. Eight children said that they would like to see more of their non-resident parent's family.

The children were asked how they got on with their 'stepparent(s)' (this included the new partner, married or not, of either parent). Sixteen children did not answer the question, 11 children spoke positively of new partners and three children mentioned uncles who acted like fathers at times.

Conclusions

With such a small sample and with such a diversity of experiences, the conclusions that can be drawn from these findings can only be tentative. One thing is clear - children are engaged in the process, they often want more information, and they often want help in ensuring that their voices are heard.

It was telling that, despite the sensitive nature of the interviews, the young people were keen to take part in the research for they believed that by doing so they would help other children 'in their situation'.

In Chapter 8, the levels of emotional and behavioural difficulties in the children are discussed and in Chapter 9 the children's recommendations on how to improve the process are given.

Summary

- Most of the 30 children who were interviewed said that they knew why they were seeing the FCWO and what the FCWO did. They liked the FCWO and thought they had been taken seriously. Some children were worried that their parents would learn about what they had said to the FCWO.

- Less than half the children thought that they had been involved in the decision-making process, although 83% would have liked to have been. Up to a half of children would have liked another family member or a friend involved. Half thought children should be allowed to go to court.

- Children described positive relationships with both parents. However, half the children were aware that their parents disagreed about contact arrangements and one third had witnessed their parents pushing or shoving in an argument. Just under a third of children said they would rather not see the parent they did not live with if this meant an end to the arguments.

8

The well-being of parents and children

The weight of evidence that youngsters with emotional disorders are likely to have similar difficulties in young adulthood will presumably put to rest any lingering notions that depressive or anxiety disorders in young people are a temporary phase. (Kovacs and Devlin, 1998, p 47)

The longitudinal research evidence suggests that [behavioural difficulties], particularly when some estimate of severity is taken into account, is the single most powerful predictor of later adjustment problems of any childhood behavior studied. (Kohlberg et al, 1984, p 132)

This chapter focuses on the children's emotional well-being and the relationship between that of the child and that of the parent. It is arguable that if judgements are made 'in the best interests of the child' these decisions should promote the child's emotional well-being.

As seen in Chapter 1, during and subsequent to the divorce process children can experience distress and adjustment problems, but *in the long term* the outcome of divorce for the majority children is comparable to that of those whose parents have never divorced. Emotional and behavioural difficulties in children have a myriad of causes, but children exposed to parental conflict after their parents' separation are particularly vulnerable to more severe problems (see Buchanan and Hudson, 2000, for a further review of this literature).

Any breakdown in a parental relationship is likely to involve distress in the parents. It is possible that the distress is more intense among those families who cannot agree the arrangements for their children. It is also possible that the court processes to sort out the arrangements may actually intensify this distress.

Why does this matter? The concern is that poor mental health in adults is linked to emotional difficulties in childhood (DoH et al, 1998). Poor mental health is also a leading cause of disability, which is likely to affect parenting capacity as well as physical health (Power et al, 1991). Of greater concern is that mental health in parents is linked to the mental health of children (Health Advisory Service, 1995).

The major concern is that such difficulties can seriously interfere with a child's life chances and have long term consequences. Not only are such children more likely to exhibit a range of problems in school and elsewhere as they grow up (Moffitt, 1990; Offord and Bennett, 1994; Champion et al, 1995; Kovacs and Devlin, 1998), they may underachieve educationally leading to disadvantage in later employment. Their relationships with family and peers can also be affected. What is more worrying is that some children will continue to have mental health and other difficulties in later life (Harrington et al, 1990; Harrington, 1992; Patterson et al, 1993).

The measures

This study is unique in that parents' and children's well-being was assessed using standardised measures both at the end of the legal proceedings related to their Section 8 application and, again, one year subsequently (see Appendix A for the methodology).

At both stages the parents were asked to complete a 12-question GHQ and a SDQ relating to their child (the one whose name came first in the alphabet if more than one child, although children of eight years or over were prioritised because they were eligible to take part in the children's interviews). In this way the final sample of completed SDQs at the first parental interview included a random assortment of first-, second- and, in some cases, third-born children. They also included a range of children of different ages. The children interviewed also completed a self-report SDQ. In the analyses, if an SDQ had been completed for a child by both parents, the score from the resident parent was used, as it was felt that they would have a greater knowledge of the child's day-to-day behaviour.

General Health Questionnaire

The GHQ is a 'state' measure, providing an indication of how much an individual feels their present state is unlike their usual state. It is recommended for studying a cohort of individuals during a process or period of stress and disruption. The questionnaire does not provide information on lifelong traits, nor does it make clinical diagnoses, rather, it focuses on breaks in normal function. Two main areas are explored: the inability to carry out normal 'healthy' functions and the appearance of new phenomena of a distressing nature (Goldberg and Williams, 1988; NFER-Nelson, 2001). Using the GHQ-12 and the Likert scoring method, a threshold of 12 was used (maximum score 36) (see 'Questions' section of NFER-Nelson, 2001).

There are some demographic and personality variables that have an effect on GHQ scores. Divorced and separated women have been shown to report an increased rate; rates are also higher for those who are unemployed (Goldberg and Williams, 1988). Social class and age do not have strong effects on GHQ scores, although some surveys show higher rates in lower social classes. In this study, 94 GHQs were completed at the time of the first interviews, and 77 at the second.

Strengths and Difficulties Questionnaire

The SDQ is a 25-item measure, of which different versions are available to be completed by young people themselves, parents or teachers. This instrument has been validated against the widely used Rutter 'A' Health and Behavioural Checklist (Goodman, 1997, 2001) and incorporates many of its

well-recognised strengths. The SDQ, however, is shorter with a positive focus and is valid for a wider age range. The measure is recommended in the *Framework for the assessment of children in need and their families* (DoH, 2000). The parent-report SDQ was used in this study, one for 4 to 16-year-olds and one for 3- to 4-year-olds. In addition 28 young children completed the self-report version at the child interview.

Scores are divided into three categories: normal, borderline and abnormal. It would be expected, in the general population, to find 80% of all children in the normal range, 10% in the borderline and 10% in the abnormal range. In a study of more than 10,000 children in the UK, the mean total score on the parent-report SDQ for all children was 8.4. Boys had a slightly higher mean at 9.1 and girls slightly lower at 7.8. Children aged 5-10 years had a marginally higher mean at 8.6 compared to 11- to 15-year-olds at 8.2 ('Scoring the SDQ' section of Goodman, 2001). As recommended by Goodman (1997), the children in this study were divided into those who had scores that fell into the normal range (less than 14) and those who fell into the borderline or abnormal range (more than 14). At the first interview stage, 56 children were reported on by one or more parent and 47 were reported on one year later.

Parental well-being

At the first interview 84% of all the parents experienced disruption to their 'normal' functioning as measured by the GHQ. Figures were very similar for mothers and fathers, applicants and respondents. A year later 38% of all parents were still experiencing emotional problems. See Figure 8.1 for a breakdown by gender and applicant/respondent.

The impact of the court process on parents

As seen in Chapter 3, although a small number of parents said that the proceedings had a negligible impact on them (and one father found it a positive experience), the vast majority described a disruptive, nerve-wracking and exhausting process, which came to dominate their lives and adversely affected their psychological and physical health.

Figure 8.1: Parents' GHQ scores

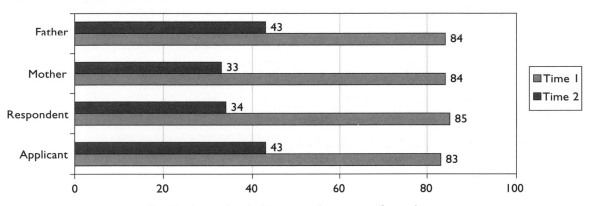

% with above threshold score indicating significant distress

"Those five months were absolutely terrible – especially the last three when I had so much legal stuff. I was absolutely knackered. I was so tired from looking after the children anyway that I was looking at them and the words weren't making sense. I got into a total state at one point. It got to the point that if a white envelope came through the door that looked like it was from the court.... I would wait for the postman and think, 'Oh no, what now?' The 'phone was ringing; it would either be the solicitor or the welfare officer. So, yes, it affected me badly." (Mother)

"I felt pretty shitty. I was on the verge of a nervous breakdown. I was on the edge of doing something very, very silly – I was on the edge of saying, 'Fuck it, I'm not going to bother at all', but I just couldn't do that. On a couple of occasions I thought, 'That's it, I'm not going to go back to court, I'm not going to fight it, I'm just going to piss off and go to France'. But there was something telling me not to do that." (Father)

"You just felt so useless in everything, you feel as if you're a zombie. You go along doing your everyday things but you're not much use to anyone and you feel that no one would notice if you had gone, sort of thing." (Mother)

These quotes indicate that some parents were struggling to cope with the normal day-to-day functions. It is unlikely that these parents had much emotional capacity left to support their children who were also distressed.

Dissatisfaction with welfare reporting process and the arrangements

Had the parents in this study benefited from the judicial processes? Some parents had apparently not benefited. Parents with a high GHQ score at the second interview were more likely than those with low scores to be dissatisfied with the welfare reporting process and with the current arrangements for the children. Of course, it could be that these parents remained distressed because they were unhappy with the current arrangements, or it could be that they had more profound problems that required another type of service. High levels of hostility and conflict were also associated with high GHQ scores.

Other factors associated with a high GHQ

As we have seen, the very high levels of parental distress at the first interview affected around eight out of ten parents. A year later four or five parents out of ten were feeling more emotionally stable. It may be that time had helped to heal the pain of their separation, but it is also possible that the court processes played a part in reducing the stresses.

However, three or four parents out of ten remained distressed. Although adult mental health problems have many causes, ongoing high scores on the GHQ were, not surprisingly, associated with more complex social situations, such as a history of domestic violence, low income and a relationship with the other parent that had not involved marriage (see Figure 8.2).

Figure 8.2: Factors associated with a high GHQ in parents at the second interview

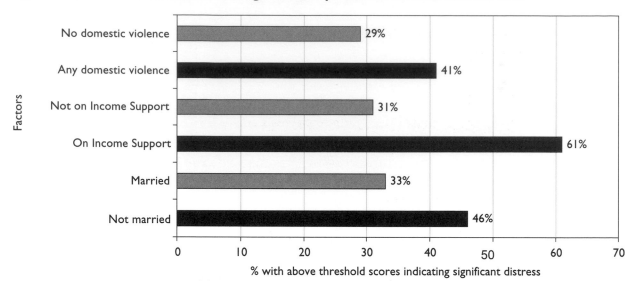

Children's well-being

"Do not forget that we are distressed too." (Child)

Of the children, 46% had borderline or abnormal SDQ scores at the first interview, indicating a significant level of emotional and behavioural difficulties (see Figure 8.3). By the second interview 53% of the children assessed fell into this bracket, but the outcomes for boys were very different to those for girls (see Figure 8.4). Although 38% of girls were still indicating significant difficulties – nearly twice that expected in the general population, the percentage of boys with emotional and behavioural difficulties had increased to 62% – three times that expected. Boys at every stage of the study were likely to show more emotional and behavioural difficulties than were girls; although this is in keeping with national trends, the differential was many times greater than that expected. Overall, younger children were more likely to show such difficulties than were older children. Although this is also in keeping with national trends the differences were, again, far greater than anticipated.

When parents were asked to say how they felt their children were doing at the first interview, their responses broadly reflected the SDQ findings: 40% of parents said that they thought that their children were doing alright; 42% reported that one or more of their children was experiencing problems; 5% reported severe difficulties. More than a quarter of the parents felt their children needed more help.

It was not feasible to collect data relating to children's well-being pre-proceedings. However, parental reports indicate that just over half were considered to be 'okay', with only a very few children considered to have severe difficulties. Moreover, children were felt to be doing better than they had been at an earlier stage, although in 14 cases things were worse.

Other factors associated with children's adjustment

There was a relationship between high levels of stress in the parent as measured by the GHQ and children's distress as measured by the parent-report SDQ. Where a parent scored above the threshold on the GHQ, over half of the children also had borderline or abnormal SDQ scores. Parental distress was particularly associated with children's emotional and behavioural well-being at the second interview a year later. Domestic violence also strongly influenced children's emotional and behavioural well-being. As can be seen in Figure 8.5, when domestic violence was an issue in the proceedings, the children involved had an SDQ score more than three times higher than the level expected in the general population.

Figure 8.3: Children with emotional or behavioural problems as measured by the SDQ (parent report) (%)

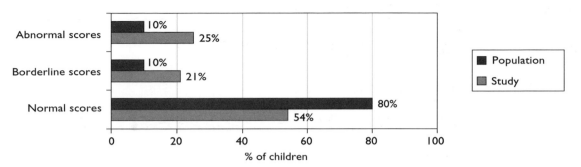

Note: At time 1, compared with general child population.

Figure 8.4: Abnormal/borderline SQD scores by gender (parent report)

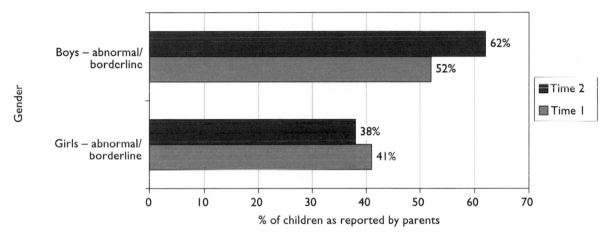

Figure 8.5: Children with borderline/abnormal SDQ scores (parent report) (%)

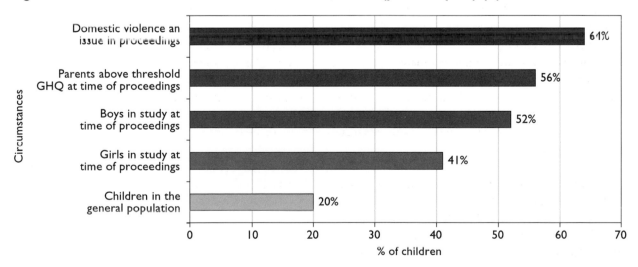

Comparison with children subject to 'care' proceedings

Although the children in this study had experienced parental separation and, often, high levels of family conflict, at least they were still living with one of their parents and were often in contact with the other. On the "Richter scale of family turmoil" (Timmis, 2000, p 2) their 'earthquake' was less catastrophic than those experienced by children who have been subject to public law proceedings. A rare opportunity to compare these groups was afforded by Harwin's study of the implementation of care plans (Harwin et al, forthcoming). The Harwin et al study used the child-report version of the SDQ on 22 children 21 months after the end of proceedings. When compared to the 28 children interviewed in this study who also used the child-report version of the SDQ, 12 months or so after the end of their proceedings, *there was no difference between the groups* (see Figure 8.6). Both groups had nearly *double* the levels of emotional and behavioural disturbance expected in the general population.

Conclusions

In this study, scores on the GHQ were remarkably high for this group of parents, even considering that generally higher scores are reported by divorced women (Goldberg and Williams, 1988). Over a year later, the scores *did* go down for many parents, but a sizeable number of mothers and fathers remained over the threshold, indicating considerable distress and that their levels of functioning had not returned to normal after this period of time.

It is highly probable that the court processes negatively impact on parents' emotional well-being. There is no precise way of establishing this, given the myriad of different events that take place while parents are involved with the court and in the following year. However, there is evidence from the parents' testimonies that the court process was very stressful, above and beyond the separation and other life events.

The relationship between parents' well-being and children's levels of emotional and behavioural difficulties was pronounced at the second interview. At both interviews, the parents reported very high levels of emotional and behavioural problems in their children. The striking comparison with the SDQ self-report scores from children in public care proceedings reveals how difficult both processes can be for children.

The emerging picture is that, if the children's well-being is to be promoted, there is a need to explore less stressful ways of helping parents with already high levels of distress, in particular those with complex problems, to sort out the arrangements for their children. The need for support services and preventative measures is discussed in Chapter 10.

Figure 8.6: SDQ scores (child report) of children in public care compared to children involved in FCWS (%)

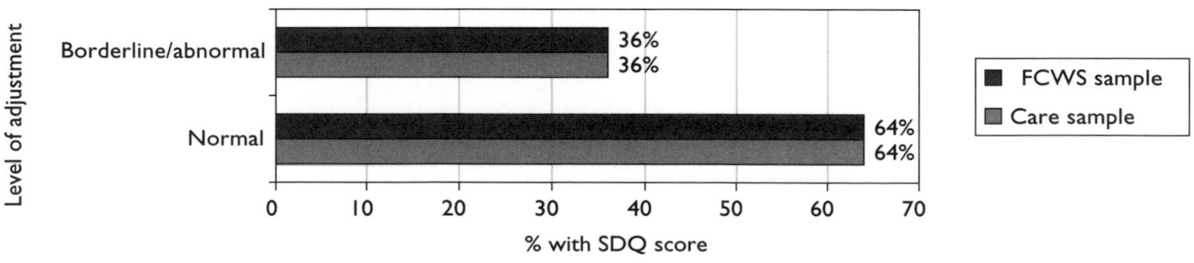

Summary

- This study is unique in that standardised measures of well-being were completed for children and parents at the end of the legal proceedings and one year later.
- At the first interview 84% of parents had scores above the GHQ threshold, indicating significant distress and disruption to normal functioning.
- A total of 46% of the children had borderline or abnormal scores on the SDQ, indicating a significant level of emotional and behavioural difficulties.
- In the year that followed proceedings, the well-being of parents improved.
- The emotional health of female children improved in the year following the proceedings, but that of male children did not.
- At the second interview there was a relationship between children's emotional and behavioural difficulties and parental dysfunction.
- Parents whose distress remained high were significantly more likely to have experienced more complex problems including domestic violence.
- The percentage of children with borderline/abnormal SDQ scores (child-report) was identical to the percentage in another study of children who had been subjects of care proceedings. This suggests that children may be as distressed in 'private' law proceedings to make arrangements for their future as in 'public' law proceedings where the state is involved because of child protection issues.

9

How to make it better – what the children and parents said

We see the centrality of the child as all-important. There will be tensions around the child, because in disputed cases the parents will hold different positions. The needs of the adult positions obscure and overwhelm the needs of the child but promoting the child's mental health remains the central issue. (Sturge and Glaser, 2000, p 616)

How to make things better – the children's views

> "Parents think it is easier for children, but in fact it is harder." (Child)

There is a growing literature of children's views on separating and divorcing parents (see O'Quigley, 1999). Many of the findings of this report reflect those seen in the Douglas et al study (in press). What is different here, however, is that these children have all been the subjects of a court welfare report. They are children living with conflict. Many of these children have developed sophisticated coping strategies for surviving in an environment where, for some, family conflict and violence has been an everyday reality.

Children took part in the study because they wanted to help other young people in their situation. Some of the most telling comments from them came at the end of the interview when they wrote down their 'top tips' for others. Children firstly gave a list of top tips for other children in their situation; secondly, top tips for parents who could not agree on the arrangements for their children; and, finally, top tips for FWCOs. These encapsulated many of the findings reported in Chapter 7.

Top tips for other children

Their ideas for other children poignantly illustrated the stress that these children experience and their need for more support.

How to cope

- Find something you like to do and the worries may go away.
- Keep in touch with friends – don't go off in loneliness.
- If you get annoyed don't lash out.
- Don't start taking drugs and alcohol just because of your position.
- Try helping a brother or sister to get through it – it might help you too.

Don't get too involved

- Don't put yourself in the arguments, don't listen that much.
- Don't let it take over your life.

A second set of suggestions illustrated how difficult it was for children to say what they wanted. They had learned to mistrust those around them. They could not always trust their parents to be honest about their wishes; they wanted to know what the FCWO was writing in the report, and many wanted some non-partisan person outside the family to provide support. There was a strong plea for more information, so that they could have more understanding and control over their situation.

Keep informed

- Try and find out everything that is going to happen beforehand.
- If you are older ask to see the FCWO's papers [report].
- Concentrate on what they are asking – if you answer questions wrong, life might be miserable forever.
- Don't think your parents will be truthful about what you want.

Say what you think

- Say what you want to the FCWO, as sometimes you can't say it to parents.
- If there is something you really don't want stick up for yourself.

Involve others

- Make your views heard; talk to your family or anyone you feel comfortable with.
- You can always speak to other people (not mum and dad).

It will be okay

- Don't think that your parents will never talk to each other again.
- You will get over it, even if it takes a long time.
- It won't change your school friends – you won't be different from other children.

Top tips for parents when they cannot agree the arrangements

Young people's advice to parents was even more direct: tell your children what is going on, argue somewhere else and don't pressurise us. They wanted parents to know the distress they were causing their children and they did not want their parents to take out their unhappiness on them.

Tell your children what is going on

- Children want to know what happens – it affects them; they should know.
- Explain in a nice, easy way – this should be in-depth with older children; younger children need an idea of where things are going.

Argue somewhere else

- Parents shouldn't argue as much; don't go to the other parent and start abusing them.
- Try not to fight when the kids are around
- Keep calm when arguing.

Don't pressurise

- Don't bribe your children.
- If a child chooses the other parent, still love them and don't get mad with them or be mean, or they will stop seeing you.
- Don't push your children to do stuff or it will backfire.
- Try not to be sad in front of the children.
- Don't smack; don't take out your frustration on the children.

Young people also wanted their parents to be more aware of their children's unhappiness, be more prepared to listen to their views and more willing to think about their children's feelings.

Remember we are distressed too

- Give children activities to do.
- Let them see as many friends as possible.
- Remember your children.
- Be happy when the children are around, even if it's not true.
- You are a parent so you should look after your kids.

Our views matter

- Some children may want to spend more time with one parent than the other.
- If a child wants to see their dad they should tell someone about it.
- Be happy for your kids if that is the decision they have made.

Think about us

- Think more about how it will affect your children than your own lives.
- Parents need to know about bad things that may be happening to their children because of their problems – I know someone who is being badly bullied.

Top tips for FCWOs

The young people also had fairly clear messages for FCWOs. Most of these comments suggest that FCWOs could be *more skilful* at communicating with children and *more sophisticated in assessing* children's wishes and feelings. Children saw the FCWO as a non-partisan person who could give them information and who could advise them about what would be likely to happen. Some children also looked to the FCWO to try and ease the conflict and stop their parents 'being nasty'.

Don't pester

- If a child says 'don't know' you should accept it.
- There should be less questions about how you are feeling etc; not too many 'feelings' questions.
- Before questioning children ask if they like drawing or if they prefer to answer questions.
- Don't ask the same question again and again and again.
- Don't pester children or they will feel uncomfortable.

Listen and speak to us in a way we can understand

- If young children are going through a problem talk to them in a child's way; some children don't really understand what you are saying but they will not say so.
- Listen to what children are saying and tell it to people who will help change things.

Reassure

- Be trustworthy.
- Answer questions as easily as you can.
- You should realise that it is not easy for children – it might be hard for them to tell you what they are thinking.
- Most children are more comfortable at home.
- You should try and understand it from the children's point of view, explain things they do not understand.

Advise and help

- Give more information.
- Tell everyone what is going to happen.
- Talk to the children and tell the parents what the children want.
- When parents are being nasty try and sort it out.

Representation of the child's interests and views

As can be seen from these top tips, children did not necessarily trust their parents to represent their views accurately. None of the children in this sample were separately represented. The majority of parents did not think representation would have helped, mainly because they considered that the FCWO was fulfilling this function.

"I would have thought that was precisely the role of the CWO." (Father)

When FCWOs were asked whether children should be separately represented none of the FCWOs thought it was necessary, typically because, they thought they fulfilled that role.

> "I believe the child was able to make his wishes and feelings known to me and that I was able to express them to the court."
>
> "I think I conveyed their position, wishes and feelings fully."

Nonetheless 17 parents (in 15 cases) thought that representation would have been useful in their particular circumstances, while another seven said they could envisage cases in which it would be helpful. Given that most parents were not 'tuned in' to the idea of representation before the question was posed and few seemed aware that it was even a remote possibility, this is a not an insignificant number.

Parents at the first interview also expressed anxieties about how their child had been assessed by the FCWO. At the second interview there was strong support for the proposition that the wishes and feelings of the child should be taken into account and that the child's interests should be paramount, but less than half felt they had been. Children generally asked for a greater say in the decision making.

How to make things better – the parents' perspective

In any judicial process, it is likely that one party will feel less happy about the outcome than the other. In this study, however, a substantial number of parents were critical of the legal process, more than half were dissatisfied with the way the welfare report was prepared, and even parents who were broadly happy with the way the decisions were made had suggestions for improving the service.

Advice and suggestions from parents fell into three categories. First, they put forward ideas for changing the way in which welfare reports are prepared. Second, they made suggestions for changing how decisions are taken about children when their parents cannot agree. Some of these involved radical changes

Anxieties about whether children's wishes and feelings were adequately represented

Parents at stage 1 interview (*n*=100)
- 31% were not confident that their child felt that they had been listened to.
- 41% said that the welfare report did not focus on their child's needs.
- 44% were not satisfied with how their child's views had been reported.
- 46% said that the child had not been seen enough times.
- 65% were dissatisfied on one or more of the above aspects.

Parents at stage 2 interview (*n*=81)
- 73% felt that the wishes and feelings of children should be taken into account.
- 43% felt that the wishes and feelings of children should be *and are* taken into account.
- 91% felt that the best interests of the child should be paramount.
- 48% felt that the best interests of the child should be *and are* paramount.

Children interviewed (*n*=30)
- More than half thought that children should be allowed to go to court; *none of them actually did.*
- More than four in five wanted to be involved in decision making; *less than half felt they were.*
- More than three quarters wanted there to be someone in court *just for them.*

to the legal process or, indeed, removing these decisions from the legal arena altogether. Finally, many parents argued that the beliefs and principles that they saw underpinning decisions taken in the family courts were fundamentally flawed. The critique of the family court belief system was mounted from two opposing positions – typically one taken by fathers and the other by mothers. In this chapter, parents make both practical and more visionary suggestions for change.

Improving the preparation of the welfare report

Based on the views expressed by parents during the first round of interviews, at the second stage, interviewees were asked if they agreed or disagreed with a series of statements about the preparation of welfare reports.

FCWOs should have more time to spend on each case

If there was one change that most parents said they would like to see, it was that FCWOs should have more time to prepare the welfare report: over three quarters supported this. Two thirds did not believe that the amount of time FCWOs had to prepare the report on their child allowed the investigation to be thorough enough.

Over half of parents would have liked the FCWO to spend more time talking with the children. They did not believe that the FCWO spent enough time with the child to gain their confidence. Some wanted their child observed over a period of time at school and at home; some would have liked to have had longer interviews themselves or for their ex-partner to be more thoroughly investigated.

FCWOs should speak to more people about the children and parents

Parents felt that other professionals who knew the child, such as schoolteachers, should be asked for their assessment. In particular, some parents suggested that other family members such as new partners and grandparents could help the FCWO to build up a realistic picture of the child and their environment.

Home visits should be done in every case

Three quarters of parents thought that children should be visited at home in every case. These parents argued that their child was more at ease at home than in an office setting and therefore better able to express their views on the decision that had to be made. They thought that it was difficult for the FCWO to assess the quality of the relationship between the child and their parent in an office and impossible to assess how the child related to other members of the household who might not be interviewed without a visit to the home.

Some parents (39%) felt strongly that home visits should be done without a prearranged appointment. For the most part these were parents who were anxious about the level of care their children received in their ex-partner's home; they believed the FCWO would only get a true picture if the visit was not planned. However, a similar number of parents thought that prearranged appointments should be made. One reason for this was that the FCWO would waste time visiting homes when no one was in.

Parents should be involved in the planning of the investigation

Nearly all parents felt that the FCWO should involve them in deciding how the investigation should be undertaken. However, over half the parents did not feel that their views had been taken into account. These parents did not wish to dictate who should be interviewed and where, but they did believe that a better decision could have been made if their views had been taken into account about where the child was seen, who brought them to the office and which other family members or professionals were involved. It was important for *all* parents that the FCWO tell them in advance what interviews they had arranged and who they would be contacting. It was also essential that the FCWO should let them know if they changed their plans. Parents should also know beforehand what documents (such as statements) the FCWO would use for their assessment.

Greater openness about the process

Several parents said they wanted a clear explanation from the FCWO of the basis on which their children's needs and their own capacity to care for their child would be assessed. They also wanted to know beforehand what to expect in the welfare report.

The importance of the past

Most parents (four out of five at the second stage interviews) did not accept that the history of their own relationship had no bearing on the assessment of what was best for their children. They rejected an exclusively future-focused approach when this had been adopted by the FCWO.

It should be easier to contact the FCWO

A substantial minority (42%) of parents did not feel able to contact the FCWO if they were concerned about the way in which the report was being prepared.

FCWOs need more training in working with children

A third of parents said that they thought FCWOs needed more training in working with children.

Ideas with mixed levels of support

Dispute resolution

Parents had very different views about the role of the FCWO in helping parents resolve their disagreements. Nearly half believed that the FCWO should help parents sort out their disagreements, but over a third felt equally strongly that this was *not* a role for the FCWO. Only one in five parents said that the FCWO had, in fact, tried to help them sort out their disagreements with their ex-partner.

Joint interviews

Of those parents who saw value in the FCWO trying to help them reach a settlement about the children, a few suggested that joint meetings with their ex-partner would have been more effective than individual meetings.

Improving the process for making decisions about children

Proceedings should be much quicker

A common theme was that proceedings carried on far too long. Many parents expressed a sense that the proceedings assumed a momentum of their own and that they felt they had no control over what happened. Given the stress induced by the proceedings for many parents, any move to shorten them could only benefit parents and children.

All hearings should be heard by the same judge

Three quarters of parents supported the idea that one judge should take responsibility for their case. A few parents had had their case reserved by a particular judge, which they appreciated. However, there were also parents who had had a bad experience in front of a judge and who welcomed the opportunity to face a different judge at a different hearing. These parents positively opposed the proposal for an allocated judge.

There should be effective and speedy remedies for breaches of a court order

Although most parents said that action should be taken by the courts if a parent breached a court order, they recognised the difficulty in finding an appropriate sanction that would not harm the child. Fines were suggested as a possible enforcement mechanism. Only three parents advocated imprisoning a parent who was in breach of an order – most recognised that the children would suffer more than the parent.

The court should check on whether their orders are being adhered to

Three quarters of parents agreed that the court, possibly through the FCWS, should visit families to find out if orders were being complied with. Some parents saw this as a way of supporting fragile arrangements. Others believed that continuing court involvement was a method of preventing an ex-partner from disregarding an order. A fifth of parents strongly disagreed with this proposal arguing that parents and children should be responsible for making decisions in light of a court order, without the intervention of an outside agency.

Gate-keeping

A few parents wanted courts to make a preliminary decision on the merits of all applications before allowing proceedings to start. They believed that their ex-partner had used the court process as a weapon in the parental battle rather than because they genuinely wanted the best for their child.

Domestic violence

Most parents wanted allegations of domestic violence to be investigated before a decision was made about contact – mothers favouring this more strongly than fathers.

A different system

Decisions about contact and residence should not be made by the courts

This was the most radical proposal made by a number of parents at the first interviews, and supported by over half at the second stage. There were several reasons advanced for having a system for resolving parents' disputes outside of the courts. First, decisions were made by people who did not know the child and were therefore unlikely to be sensitive to the child's needs. Second, the involvement of the court, in itself, worsened relationships between the parents and sometimes between parents and children: "You can't come back from court and remain friends". Third, it was damaging for children to be the focus of court proceedings.

Parents who wanted an alternative to court adjudication were generally less specific about what should replace it. Features appeared to include greater informality, the attempt to enable parents to reach an agreement and the involvement of child specialists.

However, a third of parents believed that the court was the only arena in which parents could bring their disputes if all other avenues (such as mediation) had already been tried. Indeed, some of the parents who favoured an alternative to a court system also recognised that the legal process, unsatisfactory as it was, had to provide arbitration as a last resort.

Mediation should be compulsory before the start of court proceedings

Nearly two thirds of parents agreed with this proposition, although the parents who did not agree felt strongly that mediation could not be effective if it was compulsory and would only contribute to delay.

Support and advice about children should be available to parents who separate

There was very strong support for services to help parents minimise the distress for their children when they separated. Nearly all parents believed that information should be available to parents at the point of separation to help them make the best possible decisions about the children. A similar number believed that parents should be able to seek expert advice outside the legal process about making arrangements for children. More than 90% thought that expert advice should be available once the proceedings were over. Some parents had specifically regretted that they were not able to ask for advice on problems that had arisen once the proceedings were over.

Support groups

Mothers in particular talked about their sense of isolation in going through court proceedings about their children. Some would have welcomed the opportunity to meet other parents in the same position.

Support for children

Despite the high levels of distress exhibited by many children (see Chapters 7 and 8), most parents did not believe that their child needed help from outside the family. However, a few did think that an advice, counselling or therapeutic service should be available to children whose parents had separated, particularly if there were legal proceedings.

Gender-biased critiques of 'the system'

Beyond changes in how welfare reports were prepared and legal proceedings were conducted, some parents argued powerfully that the principles and assumptions that lay behind the decisions of the courts and the advice of the FCWOs were fundamentally flawed. Generally, fathers mounted one critique and mothers another. It was in their critiques of what they believed to be the assumptions operating in the family justice system that the views of mothers and fathers diverged most clearly.

Given the overlap between resident parents and mothers, and non-resident parents and fathers, it was not possible to know whether the different perspectives reflected gender or parental residence status. Indeed, the only father who was a resident parent in a contact dispute used the same arguement as many mothers to criticise 'the system'. A study involving a far larger number of resident fathers and non-resident mothers would be needed to isolate the effects of gender from residence status.

Shared care

A distinction needs to be drawn between disputes that are, in essence, about 'shared' parenting and those which are about the need for a parent to have contact with their child. Many of the fathers believed in the principle of shared care, which would allow their child to have a fully developed relationship with both their parents. They rejected the concept of a resident and non-resident parent. They argued that children need their father to be as fully involved with them as their mother. A balanced relationship required that the child spent more or less the same amount of time with both parents and that they both had similar responsibilities for nurturing, discipline and taking decisions about health and education. These fathers favoured 'shared care' arrangements giving equality of status to both parents. They disputed the assumption

that children need one primary carer and one primary place of residence. They also disputed the assumption that shared parenting can only work well for a child if there is a low level of conflict between the parents.

> "There's not much recognition in the court system or the FCWS of shared parenting. It is supposed to be an integral part of the Children Act and is seen as highly desirable ... but they do not see that as a priority. They seek to take residence with the mother as the key issue. [Shared parenting] is highly beneficial. Even cases where separated parents are not in harmony about everything – the children in shared parenting benefit enormously compared to those who do not have shared parenting." (Father)

The mothers who resisted their ex-partner's bid for shared care argued that their child needed one home and one parent to be primarily responsible for their daily care and for taking major decisions. They feared that their child would be confused and unsettled by the different cultures and expectations in two different households and believed that shared care would expose the child to daily parental conflict. For the many mothers who had struggled to provide stability and security for their children, often at great emotional cost, their ex-partner's attempt to take on a fuller parenting role was experienced as a threat to their own ability to parent effectively.

But, as was seen in Chapter 7, many children valued their father's role. Nearly three quarters felt they got on really well with their dad; nearly two thirds felt they could talk to him about things that bothered them; more than eight out of ten knew that their dad was interested in how they got on school and had a really good time when they were with him. Only one in five were scared of their dad and only one in ten resented the time they spent with him.

> "I think that, for the children ... they have a busy school week, they have friends and a routine they have established with me when their father was never around at weekends. Now they are whisked off to Wales. They never spend any time at home when they are with him. When they are with me they spend it in a home – a normal existence – boring as it might be sometimes." (Mother)

The right to contact

The second broad category of disputes was about the need for all children to have a relationship with both their biological parents. The fathers in these disputes, who had all limited their applications to contact, believed that children's emotional well-being depended on them spending time with the parent they were not living with. They had learnt that case law (see Chapter 1) gave the child the right to a relationship with both parents rather than giving the parent a right to a relationship with their child. At an emotional level, however, the distinction between the child's and the parent's rights did not make much sense. These fathers were desperate to maintain a relationship currently under stress, or to see the children that they had lost touch with or never known. They argued either that biological parenthood was in itself a reason for having contact or that limitations should be confined to severe domestic violence or child abuse. Fatherhood was an unconditional state.

"I think it makes a difference if you are a man ... I felt at a disadvantage. I had to prove I was a capable reliable sort of person just because I was male and I didn't have any other rights even though I was the father. I felt quite angry about that – that I was starting from the point of view of nothing really, rather than having rights to see one's child and then someone trying to take that away from you. I had to fight to acquire that and that was the wrong way round. If [mother] didn't want me to see him perhaps she should have to file for an order to stop me." (Father)

The mothers in these disputes argued that the status of parent should be earned by demonstrating parenting behaviour. It was conditional on emotional and material commitment over time to the child and on support to the mother in her parenting role. According to mothers domestic violence and child abuse were evidence that a biological parent was not necessarily a 'real' parent. They believed that children did not benefit from contact with a man who had not shown parenting qualities and the history of the father's relationship with both mother and child was therefore of critical importance in assessing the value of contact to the child. Many of these mothers believed that children whose fathers did adopt a parenting role benefited from contact with them and wished that their own children's father had shown the same qualities. They opposed either increased or, in some cases, any contact because of defective parenting by their ex-partner.

"My personal opinion is that he doesn't give a damn about the children. He only wants to see them to annoy me. Fathers may have rights but also responsibilities which he has not carried out. They only look to rights and not responsibilities." (Mother)

Beliefs

To a large extent, the disputes that focused on 'shared parenting' and those on the 'right' to contact are both about two sets of opposing beliefs. The arguments of both mothers and fathers are equally persuasive and compelling. There is little research evidence specifically relating to children whose parents have applied for 1989 Children Act orders which supports either side in the argument for shared parenting or for the right to contact.

At the time the research was undertaken, the decisions taken by the court were as belief-based as the arguments put forward by the parents. Court decisions are based on case law, rules of thumb and the personal views of judges in a particular case; they are not evidence-based (Davis and Pearce, 1999). This is partly because there is little research of direct relevance to the decisions being made but, more significantly, because legal decisions are of necessity broad-based and self-referential (King and Piper, 1995).

As many of the parents were keenly aware, the principles and assumptions which lie behind court decisions are not gender neutral. Although, as outlined, ideas may now be changing, all the evidence shows that mothers are overwhelmingly awarded residence and that fathers will only be given residence in exceptional circumstances. Shared residence orders are rarely made and, again, only in exceptional situations. Court decisions in residence cases suggest that professionals in the family justice system believe, with mothers, that children do better with a 'primary carer' and reject fathers' arguments for 'shared parenting'.

On the other hand, in contact disputes support has been given to fathers. As described in Chapter 1, unless there are clear safety reasons in relation to the child or mother, contact has been seen as both beneficial to the child and the child's 'right'. Even where there are concerns about the safety of the mother or the child, the consultation paper on contact and domestic violence (Advisory Board on Family Law, 2000) and relevant judgments (Re V (contact: domestic violence), Re M (contact: domestic violence), Re H (contact: domestic violence) [2000] 2 FLR 334 and Re L (a child) (contact: domestic violence [2000] 2 FLR 404 (2000) 4 All ER 609 [2000] 2 FLR 334) make it clear that contact should be established if it can be done so safely. Violence to the child or the mother does not in itself challenge the assumption that contact is beneficial to the child.

In these contact disputes, the professionals in the family justice system broadly support the fathers' 'right to contact' position. The mothers' argument that contact will only be useful to a child if the father has demonstrated parenting qualities is largely discounted. But fathers in contact disputes could still be disappointed – even if their application for contact was granted, they saw the courts as impotent in enforcing contact against a mother who was determined that it should not take place.

In the first stages of this research it was puzzling that mothers and fathers *both* strongly believed that court decisions had a systematic gender bias, and that the bias was against their own gender. If the argument that court decisions are belief-based is accepted and, furthermore, that in residence applications they tend to support mothers and in contact decisions support fathers, it becomes clear why both fathers and mothers can, with equal passion, believe that the courts are institutionally biased against them.

Summary

- Children gave helpful advice for other children, for parents and for FCWOs in order to help other young people in a similar situation.
- Parents, like their children, believed that children's voices should be heard and carry weight, but they had mixed views as to whether or not this had happened in practice.
- Parents made suggestions for improving the process for preparing welfare reports and, more generally, for making decisions about children in Section 8 applications.
- 'The system' was criticised by both mothers and fathers from different gender-based perspectives.

10

Implications for policy and practice

The aims of the new Children and Family Court Advisory and Support Service (CAFCASS) are:

- Improve the decision making for some of the most vulnerable children in society – those whose care is under review and those whose parents are separating and cannot agree amicable custodial arrangements.
- Enable children to participate effectively in the decision-making process and communicate their wishes effectively to the courts.
- 'Children First': set up a unified Children and Family Court Advisory and Support Service. (CAFCASS, 2000)

Reflected in this study are the views of parents and children involved in contested court proceedings. Parents and children gave up their time and shared intimate and painful experiences because they wanted policy makers and practitioners to understand how users of the service felt. Many wanted policy and practice to change.

All research must be seen in the context of its limitations. One of the strengths of this study is that the families and children who took part are broadly representative of those families coming to FCWS in the three areas. The major limitation is that there was no control group, so that we cannot say *for sure* whether the perceptions of these parents and children were related specifically to their involvement with the FCWS or more generally to the process of separation and divorce. A further limitation is that the numbers of parents and children involved were too small for more complex statistical analyses, so caution needs to be used in interpreting the findings. Nonetheless, the researchers took away seven powerful messages from the interviews:

Key findings

- *Parents – whether they were mothers or fathers, applicants or respondents – were highly distressed* (at the first interview 84% were above the threshold indicating significant distress on the GHQ). Parental distress was, in part, related to the court proceedings and to some extent was alleviated once proceedings were over.
- *Children were highly distressed* (46% had significant emotional and behavioural difficulties and this rose to 64% where domestic violence was an issue in the proceedings). Also, for boys, the distress did not alleviate once proceedings were over and for girls it remained high. Child distress, particularly at the second interview, was linked to distress in the resident parent. The children who were interviewed at this time reported distress *almost twice* the level expected in the general population – a rate comparable with that of children who had been made subject to care orders.
- *While children generally liked the FCWO, many did not feel their voices had been heard by the court process or by their parents.* Of those interviewed, eight out of ten children wanted to be involved in the decision-making process but only four out of ten felt they had been. Only a third of the children were happy with the decision.
- *More than half the parents were dissatisfied with the welfare reporting process.*
- *Almost nine out of ten parents expressed some criticism of the court process.*
- *Only a quarter of the parents were completely satisfied with the arrangements a year later.*
- *Certain groups of parents were more dissatisfied with the overall process than others.* While satisfaction with welfare reporting was principally linked to outcome and initial expectations, certain groups were particularly dissatisfied.

- *Families in which parents cannot agree the arrangements for their children may have complex social and emotional needs* that may require other types of services.

The implications of these findings are considered below.

Parental distress

Parental distress was, at least partly, attributable to the stress of litigation. Given the emotional costs as well as the financial costs of proceedings, it makes sense to explore other ideas that may encourage more parents to sort out the arrangements for themselves before coming to court. Indeed, as discussed in Chapter 9, this is what many parents wanted. While the results of the mediation pilots might be regarded as disappointing in some respects (Clisby et al, 2000), this research does support the general thrust of government policy to encourage mediated settlements.

It is recognised that some families will always need the courts. The research suggests, however, that negotiations within the court process are likely to prove a less stressful experience for parents than going to a full hearing, and that negotiations prior to the day of the court hearing are likely to produce more acceptable outcomes.

Child distress

The findings about child distress that occurs when parents cannot agree the arrangements for their children reflect much of the research on children's adjustment post-parental separation as outlined in Chapter 1. Even so, the high levels of child emotional and behavioural problems found, and the increase in the SDQ scores among boys one year after the proceedings had ended were surprising. Emotional and behavioural difficulties in childhood can be associated with long-term difficulties throughout childhood and into adult life (Buchanan and Hudson, 2000). It is now well recognised that children in public care carry a significant risk of later mental health problems (Cheung and Buchanan, 1997). To find that the children interviewed in this study reported similar levels of maladjustment to a sample of children recently subject to care orders was

astonishing and raises concern about the future well-being of this far larger number of children subject to private law proceedings. Under Section 17 of the 1989 Children Act, children with emotional and behavioural problems qualify as children 'in need' and, as such, they are entitled to support services. The findings here suggest that children whose parents cannot agree the arrangements for them should be regarded as potential children 'in need' and therefore be entitled to services to enable their needs to be met.

Hearing children's voices

One of the key themes in the children's interviews was their wish to be more involved in the decisions that were central to their lives. Ensuring that they have access to good information from an early stage in the separation process may go some way to meeting this need. Their wish to have someone 'just for them' involved in the decision-making process might be partially met by them nominating another member of the family, such as a grandparent. Ensuring that FCWOs, in their new incarnation as Child and Family Reporters (CFRs), develop their skills in assessing children's wishes and feelings, and allowing them more time to do so, should also help. The new Court Amendment Rules (LCD, 2001a) also require CFRs to "notify the child of the contents of his [sic] report" (p 9) in light of the child's age and understanding. The child should be told how their own views will be conveyed and what recommendations are being made in the report. Children should therefore have a clear idea of what is being said on their behalf and what arrangements are being proposed by the CFR. They will at least know if their views have been accurately represented and they should have an understanding of what weight has been given to them.

Is this enough? In an increasingly rights-based culture the question of whether the rights of children subject to private law proceedings are being adequately protected by the current provisions is likely to be raised. The new Rules indicate that the CFR should "consider whether the child should be made a party to the proceedings" (2.11). The President of the Family Division has indicated that she would like to see children separately represented more often.

Many of the parents in this study saw the FCWO acting in a representational capacity, indeed, so did the welfare officers themselves. In the sense that the FCWO is there to make a recommendation to the court in order to promote the child's interests, this is true. The FCWO should also act as a conduit through which the child's wishes and feelings are conveyed to the court. Representation, however, is much more than this, as can be seen by comparing the role of the FCWO in a private law case with that of a guardian ad litem in public law (Hunt and Lawson, 1999).

Such a comparison reveals the hitherto relatively weak and marginal position of the FCWO in seeking to safeguard the child's interests, although the position of the CFR has been strengthened by the new court regulations issued with the creation of CAFCASS. CFRs are now able to commission expert evidence and there may be scope for CFRs to participate increasingly in negotiations on the child's behalf or to be more frequently present in court. There may also be a role for CFRs in assisting the court to manage the progress of the case in the child's interests.

CFRs are also now required to consider whether the child should be separately represented and advise the court accordingly. This change is to be welcomed. One must be wary, however, of seeing representation as a panacea. The problems families were bringing to the court were not essentially legal problems and their resolution does not depend fundamentally on legal solutions.

Dissatisfaction with the welfare reporting process

Possible explanations for the high rate of dissatisfaction with the process of welfare reporting (56% of parents) were discussed in Chapter 5. In any adversarial process at least one party is likely to be critical and, in a system which tries to reach settlement by compromise, both parties are likely to achieve rather less than they hoped. Nonetheless, the criticisms voiced about the welfare reporting process raise practice issues for the new service (CAFCASS).

More extensive assessment of the needs of children

The change most widely supported by parents was that more time should be devoted to the assessment of individual children's needs and to the ability of their parents to meet those needs. Some parents also questioned the ability of the FCWO to assess the children's needs or criticised the assessment as being subjective.

A better assessment would require more time to be spent with children and their parents and, often, for more information to be gathered from other family members and professionals. More training in assessment skills may be needed. Practitioners might also find it helpful to make use of standardised assessment measures such as those used in the *Framework for the assessment of children in need and their families* (DoH, 2000). The Goodman SDQ (Goodman, 1997, 2001) is now included in the *Framework for the assessment* tools. If the parent report as well as the child report (if the child is old enough) is used for all children referred to the service, it will give a measure of how the child is thriving in the current situation.

Improving communication with children

As noted earlier, children generally 'liked' the FCWO but, in some cases, did not feel able to communicate with them about what they really wanted. Some parents also questioned the skills of the welfare officer in ascertaining the child's wishes. Again it should be possible to increase the skills of the new CFRs through further training. The quiz used in this study, developed from work originally undertaken by Douglas et al (in press), also proved a non-threatening yet effective way of enabling children to express their feelings.

Individual, not standardised treatment

A very clear finding in this study is that it was hard to generalise the views of one child to all the children in the same family. Interviews with children gave some vivid examples of how different children cope differently with the same family situation. Most children wanted an opportunity to be seen by the

FCWO independently and do not want to be seen as part of a family group or with a parent or parents; children also wanted to be seen individually rather than with their brothers or sisters. Parents also complained about being treated as 'cases' not people and of formulaic responses to their individual situations.

Making the process more open

In public law, there has been considerable research to suggest that 'working in partnership' with parents, even in highly disputed child protection cases, produces better outcomes for children. Under the 1989 Children Act this is essential as parents retain 'parental responsibility' for their children in all cases other than adoption. Although there has been considerable discussion on what 'working in partnership' means (see Buchanan, 1994), it is generally felt to convey the concept of a more 'open' system in which information is shared, the professional worker is honest about what may happen, and parents have a role in planning the assessment and, as far as possible, in the decision making. In these highly fraught private law cases, parents were asking for a more open approach, in which they were informed about what was happening and consulted about the process.

Many parents were dissatisfied with the court process

Almost nine in ten parents expressed some criticism of the court process and 43 were entirely negative. Since the focus of this research was on welfare reporting, the interviews with parents did not, in the main, specifically investigate many aspects of the process and responses to general questions were very varied. However, there were some common themes. First, almost all parents who had been through a contested court hearing were negative about the experience. Their views were strikingly reminiscent of those of parents involved in public law proceedings, despite the difference in context. One might deduce, therefore, that parents would welcome a process that made them feel less excluded, intimidated and dehumanised. Since parents also commented, both negatively and positively, on the approach of the individual judge, it would appear that

individual practice could make some difference to these perceptions. Careful selection and training of family judges and magistrates is therefore key.

Most parents would also value a greater degree of judicial continuity, again, as did parents in public law proceedings (Hunt et al, 1999). Above all, they would like the proceedings to be concluded more expeditiously. Both of these have implications for public policy and resources as well as for local practice in case allocation and case management.

Indicators of parental dissatisfaction with the overall process

The best predictor of satisfaction with the overall process was how parents felt about the outcome of the court proceedings. Significant differences among other groupings were hard to establish because of the small numbers involved, but, nonetheless, the overall direction is worth noting.

Figure 10.1 gives a cumulative picture of parental satisfaction levels at three stages of the process: reaction to the outcome of proceedings (block one), satisfaction with the welfare reporting process (block two) and satisfaction with the process as measured 12 months later (block three). As in previous chapters, Figure 10.1 explores the levels of satisfaction by different categories of parent. It shows that, for most groups, the cumulative satisfaction score was less than 50%. Only parents with normal GHQ scores, whose children had normal SDQ scores or where there was no fear at the start of the proceedings (domestic violence) were more than 50% satisfied on the basis of the cumulative scores.

At the top of the figure, among the less satisfied groups of parents were those who were black, those who still feared their ex-partner because of previous domestic violence, those who had not been previously married and those on Income Support. Many of these parents may have more complex social and emotional problems.

In this overall matrix, it is possible to see which part of the process played the greatest part in the differentials seen. Much of the dissatisfaction of black parents, for example, was related to the outcome from the court proceedings (the first block on the bar

Figure 10.1: Overall parental satisfaction with court outcome and preparation of welfare report 12 months later

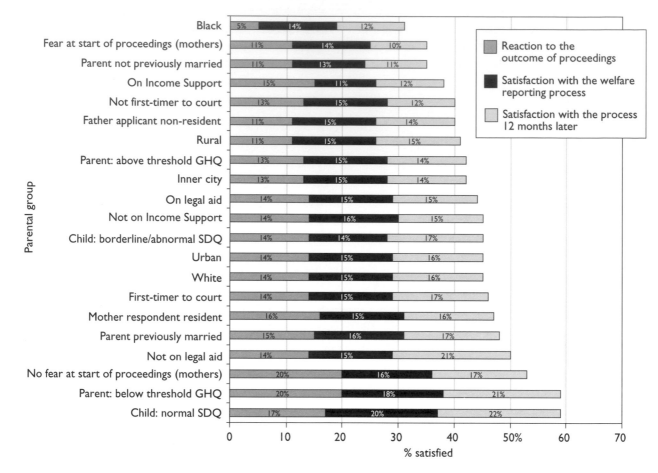

Note: GHQ = General Household Questionnaire; SDQ = Strengths and Difficulties Questionnaire

chart). One possible explanation for this is that, in this sample, black parents were more likely to be involved in cases where all contact was being opposed, either in principle or because of the child's objections. Since these are the disputes which are probably least open to compromise, both parents may be dissatisfied: mothers because their opposition to contact may not be sympathetically heard; fathers because, even if the court is supportive, contact cannot be enforced in practice.

Of course, other explanations are possible and it will be important for CAFCASS to explore why black parents, as well as other socially disadvantaged groups (such as those on Income Support and those on legal aid), appear to be less satisfied with the service.

The importance of domestic violence in disputes about children is now being recognised by the family justice system. The fact that the second most

dissatisfied group of parents in the study were mothers who were still afraid of their partners at the start of proceedings, means that this issue must remain a high priority for CAFCASS as well as the judiciary.

The dilemma for those seeking to promote the 'best interests of the child' is how to balance the potential benefits from non-resident parent involvement against the potential dangers to the resident parent and the child, and the emotional costs to the child of ongoing conflict and violence. Mothers who have experienced domestic violence may be fearful both for their own safety and that of their children. This study has also confirmed that there is a very strong relationship between family conflict and domestic violence on the one hand and children's emotional and behavioural distress on the other. In Chapter 7, it was seen that nearly three quarters of the children had heard their parents shouting at one another and more than a third had actually witnessed physical violence, while one in five were actually scared of their dad. The report to the Lord Chancellor on domestic violence and child contact (LCD, 2000b) summarises the importance attached to this issue by the family justice system and the concern that the issue is not being fully addressed by the courts. The LCD report recommends good practice guidelines and continuing training for the officers of CAFCASS and the judiciary.

It is doubtful whether these measures alone can safeguard victims of domestic violence. The contact centres, which are now available in most large towns, have an important role to play in helping children maintain, in a secure setting, a relationship with a non-resident parent who may have been violent to the resident parent. However, more could be done to help the victims and perpetrators. There are now effective treatment programmes for perpetrators and attendance on a programme could be made a condition of contact. In some cases, however, it may have to be accepted that the potential benefits to the child of contact are outweighed by the risks.

It will also be noted from Figure 10.1 that non-resident applicant fathers were more dissatisfied with the process and outcome of welfare reporting than resident respondent mothers. In part, this may have been because they came to the court with high, possibly unrealistic expectations, which were subsequently dashed. Better information for all parents about what the judicial process can, and cannot achieve, might have reduced their disappointment somewhat.

Very often, however, these fathers were not so much criticising the welfare officer as an individual, but as the representative of a system which they believed discriminated against fathers who wanted to play a significant part in their children's lives. They had difficulty in gaining greater involvement with their children in spite of legislation that ostensibly encourages the continuing involvement of both parents post-separation.

It is not hard to see that these fathers have a point; indeed, some of the research findings lend weight to their arguments. It is harder to see what can be done. Certainly it is important to ensure, through training, that legal and welfare practitioners are not basing their decisions on out-moded notions such as

maternal preference. But, in a society in which women still tend to be the primary carers, it is likely that children will remain with their mother on separation. The sad reality for non-resident fathers is that children's available time is limited, does not increase on separation and, as they get older, gets more and more taken up with school, friends and activities away from both parents.

It might be possible to enact legislation, as some of the fathers in this study argued, which presumes that children would divide their time more or less evenly between both parents on separation and ensure, through a public education campaign, that parents are aware of what is expected. But, unless parents live nearby, time-sharing is unlikely to be practicable. And would this be in the best interests of the children anyway?

As yet there is little research on shared parenting in circumstances in which parents are in conflict. The recent decision in Re D may herald a slight change of approach, which could mean that more shared residence orders are made in situations of relatively high conflict. Research would be needed to assess the effect on children of such arrangements.

The consultation paper on the enforcement of contact (LCD, 2001b) may also be helpful in producing more effective ways of dealing with 'intractable' contact disputes – another source of dissatisfaction for fathers – who may find that the court is supportive of their application for contact but is unwilling or unable to enforce the orders it makes. The approach suggested by the paper of facilitating contact rather than punishing resident parents for non-compliance with court orders would seem to be the right one.

Developing preventive services

In public law where the state intervenes to promote the well-being of children, there is a strong emphasis on 'prevention' and local authority social services departments have been encouraged to offer family support services to families, rather than move too quickly along the route of child protection and court intervention. This study has demonstrated the distress experienced by children whose parents resort to the law to 'settle' their disputes. It is considered that their distress and that of their parents too, might be minimised if a comprehensive preventive strategy were also implemented in these private law disputes.

Prevention is generally held to have three tiers: primary, secondary and tertiary. Welfare reporting and the court process – the subject of this study – are located at the tertiary level, thus, further ideas for improving the capacity of CAFCASS and the courts to act in a preventive capacity are considered after the concepts of primary and secondary prevention have been explored.

Primary prevention

Primary prevention is about providing services to all, regardless of their present need. The aim is to promote better health by reducing the overall prevalence of a particular health hazard. This is usually undertaken through education. In this case, the focus of primary prevention would be an education programme to inform children and parents how better to survive parental separation and divorce.

The parents in this study were strongly in favour (96%) of information being available to them at the point of separation. They needed information on how to talk to their children about separation and divorce, how to recognise their children's distress and how to help them avoid the more damaging aspects of separation and divorce, and strategies to resolve conflicts with the ex-partner. Although the 'information meetings' which were such a crucial part of the 1996 Family Law Act will now not be implemented, this study supports the original rationale for devising a mechanism to assist parents who have decided to separate by ensuring access to appropriate information.

Findings from the research on the pilot information meetings (Walker, 2001) give valuable ideas about how information can better be communicated to parents and children. One of the messages from this evaluation is that information needs to be available *before* parents become actively embroiled in battles over contact or residence:

The information about children struck a chord with most parents. Over 80 per cent said that the information about how children feel had been useful, and 65 per cent had

found the information useful.... It sometimes served to remind parents to consider the needs of their children. In a few cases it encouraged parents to change their behaviour or their arrangements for children....

Information may be of limited relevance and use for parents actively engaged in battles over contact or residence. Parents in these circumstances found information encouraging them to be co-operative difficult to put into practice.... Nevertheless, at the time of our follow-up interviews some 5-7 months after they had attended the information meeting, 63 per cent of attendees said they could talk to their partner about what was going on, and the younger the child the more likely it was that channels of communication between parents were open. (Walker, 2001, p 49)

The evaluation of the information meetings showed that, for parents experiencing domestic violence, 66% of women and 52% of men indicated that they were better informed about where to get help.

Information for children is also clearly crucial. This research supports the findings of other studies (Lyon et al, 1999; Douglas et al, in press) that children need information about how to handle their situation and how to cope. These information leaflets should be widely available through CAFCASS, as well as through solicitors and advice bureaux. The leaflets need to be written in age-appropriate language for different age groups or in formats that parents can use as a discussion tool with younger children. They also need to be translated into the first language of different ethnic groups.

Another message from the evaluation of the information meetings (Walker, 2001) is that leaflets given to parents to pass to their children do not often get to the children: the evaluation found that only 16% of parents actually passed them on. Focus groups with children showed that children wanted their parents to talk to them about their situations, but parents found it difficult. It may be that information for children has to come from other sources: through schools, on the Internet and through contact centres.

Schools could be involved more in helping children and young people. In the United States there is a well-validated programme: the Children of Divorce Intervention Program (Pedro-Caroll and Cowen,

1985). These programmes take place from primary school through to adolescence. The aim is to create a supportive group environment where children can share experiences, clarify misconceptions and develop skills to cope with changes. These programmes have proved very successful in improving children's behaviour and competence. Parents report better home adjustment, communication and a reduction in divorce-related concerns.

Secondary prevention

Secondary prevention should occur when parents have begun to experience difficulties in the separation process. The aim would be to help families come to the best adjustment in their new situation. Mediation, legal advice and counselling all have a role to play here. Additional services might include drop-in centres in which parents could access information and advice, support groups for mothers, fathers and children, and programmes for victims and perpetrators of domestic violence.

Hawthorne et al (in progress) at the University of Cambridge, are currently undertaking a research study of services and interventions for children experiencing divorce and family change. This should provide very useful information about the nature, distribution and effectiveness of services and facilitate the development of a national strategy that this research suggests is so important.

CAFCASS should clearly play an important part in developing this strategy and perhaps in orchestrating or even providing some services. The stumbling block is likely to be money. In the short term, resources would need to be increased but, in the longer term, if this reduced the number of families coming before the courts in each area, savings would be generated within the system. While appreciating that organisations tend to be principally concerned with their own budgets, such 'joined-up thinking' is clearly necessary.

Tertiary prevention

The aim of this third level of prevention would be to provide more effective help to the troubled families who do come to court and to prevent them

returning to court again and again. The findings from this research suggest that many families who come to the FCWS may benefit from a more *therapeutic* service rather than one which is primarily forensic.

Many of the families coming before the courts in private law disputes have complex needs. There were very high levels of reported domestic violence or fear of violence among the families in this study and more concerns about parenting than would be expected in the general population. A third of cases involved drug or alcohol abuse or mental illness. Moreover, where there has been a high level of ongoing conflict, it is likely that a satisfactory outcome from the children's point of view will require both parents to modify their beliefs, their understanding and ultimately their behaviour. While the authority of the law may encourage such shifts, and indeed may be a necessary motivating force, in itself it is unlikely to be sufficient.

The general proposition of the consultation paper *Making contact work* (LCD, 2001b) is for a more therapeutic, less legalistic court. Lord Justice Thorpe has already questioned whether the investment of public funds in therapeutic services might not produce greater benefit than a similar investment in litigation (see Re L, Re V, Re M, Re H).

A range of therapeutic services would need to be provided for both parents and children. Cognitive-behavioural techniques have proved useful and effective therapy in a range of disorders (Alford and Beck, 1997) and there is an emerging literature which suggests that the techniques are useful in cases of family conflict (Epstein and Schlesinger, 2000). Spillane-Grieco (2000) refers to a case study that successfully used cognitive-behavioural techniques with a family involved in a high-conflict divorce. Such work may prove to be valuable in enabling parents to make the shift in perspective that will often be necessary if their disputes are ever to be resolved.

Most therapeutic services could only be voluntary. However, court-ordered services, which are not uncommon in other jurisdictions, should not be ruled out. Much could be learned from other legal systems.

Evaluated pilot studies using different techniques and levels of resources could be set up to determine the most effective way of assessing children's needs and fostering belief and behaviour change in parents.

CAFCASS will have to have a role in developing and orchestrating, if not directly providing, these services. It is also suggested that CAFCASS practitioners themselves could take on a more therapeutic, less investigative role. Families do not necessarily need highly specialist psychiatric or psychological services; high quality social work input may be more appropriate and just as effective. While this does not mean that the role would be no longer investigative – at the end of the day the court may still have to make an adjudication and needs information on which to base this – it would not be restricted to investigation.

An essential part of tertiary prevention would also be that services are available to families after the court proceedings are over, whether this involves access to occasional advice, the ongoing involvement of the court reporter or continuing specialist therapy. The role and funding of Family Assistance Orders – the only way at the moment whereby the court can keep a FCWO involved with the family – needs to be reviewed.

Finding out what works

In other services there is considerable emphasis on developing both effective and cost-effective services. At this stage in the development of CAFCASS large numbers of children are involved at considerable cost in what could be seen as a life-changing social experiment with no proven efficacy. On ethical, humanitarian and economic grounds, if new services are to be developed, more needs to be known about what works or what types of inventions are most likely to lead to an improvement in the emotional well-being of the children and their parents.

In order to assess what works there needs to be some agreement about desired outcomes. All participants, parents and professionals in the family justice system agree that the best interests of the child should be paramount. The problem arises in trying to operationalise 'best interests'. This study suggests that a key component is the child's emotional well-being.

Further work needs to be done on determining desired outcomes for children and then in assessing the interventions most likely to produce these outcomes. The creation of CAFCASS, which has inherited a system of different practices in different areas, offers the scope for natural comparative trials. CAFCASS is also in the position to commission controlled trials designed to establish which interventions are most effective in terms of producing the best outcomes for children.

The future

The purpose of this study was to find out from parents and children what they felt about the preparation of the welfare report and how they experienced the court's involvement. In many ways, the findings reflect those of other studies on post-divorce factors and child adjustment outlined in Chapter 1:

> *War is not too strong a metaphor to apply to the experiences of some who divorce ... men and women are vulnerable to self-doubt, feelings of purposelessness, illness, hardship, isolation and censure ... the interaction of those inside and outside the family during the process of divorce may generate behaviour which neither side would condone in ordinary circumstances. (Clulow and Vincent, 1987, pp 1-3)*

Despite this, the *very high levels of distress* identified in this study, affecting more than seven in eight parents engaged in the process, be they mothers or fathers, resident or non-resident parents, was unexpected.

Similarly, the very high levels of distress seen in the children, with a higher percentage of boys in distress a year later, was a matter for concern. Kelly's summary of findings from studies that have largely been undertaken in the United States could equally well be applied to the findings of this study:

> *... such findings emphasize the need for divorce interventions and legal processes that will promote cooperation and reduce ongoing conflict. (Kelly, 2000, p 15)*

The development of CAFCASS provides an opportune time to find new ways of doing just this. The challenge is that whatever is done must improve the emotional well-being of children who are involved in this process. Henry Kempe who 'rediscovered' child abuse and the 'battered baby syndrome' neatly balanced the rights of the parents against the rights of the child. One of his concerns was that the procedures for child protection, in aiming to preserve the rights of the parents, resulted in further abuse to the child. This quotation can be paraphrased to represent the concerns raised by this research:

> *We do not mean that the parents do not deserve treatment [in this case, the full judicial process]. What we mean is that the child should not be used as the instrument of treatment ... there must be a more civilised way. (Kempe and Kempe, 1978, pp 128-31)*

References

Advisory Board on Family Law (1999) *A consultation paper on contact between children and violent parents: The question of parental contact in cases where there is domestic violence*, London: Lord Chancellor's Advisory Board on Family Law, Children Act Sub-Committee.

Advisory Board on Family Law (2000) *A report to the Lord Chancellor on the question of parental contact in cases where there is domestic violence*, London: Lord Chancellor's Advisory Board on Family Law, Children Act Sub-Committee.

Advisory Board on Family Law (2001) *Making contact work*, London: Lord Chancellor's Advisory Board on Family Law, Children Act Sub-Committee.

Alford, B.A. and Beck, A.T. (1997) *The integrative power of cognitive therapy*, New York, NY: The Guildford Press.

Amato, P.R. and Gilbreth, J.G. (1999) 'Non-resident fathers and children's well-being: a meta-analysis', *Journal of Marriage and the Family*, vol 61, no 3, pp 557-73.

Amato, P.R. and Keith, B. (1991) 'Parental divorce and the well-being of children: a meta-analysis', *Psychological Bulletin*, no 110, pp 26-46.

Bailey-Harris, R., David, G., Barron, J. and Pearce, J. (1998) 'Monitoring private law applications under the Children Act: Research report to the Nuffield Foundation', Unpublished, Department of Law, University of Bristol.

Bainham, A. (1998a) 'Changing families and changing concepts – reforming the language of family law', *Child and Family Law Quarterly*, vol 10, no 1, pp 1-15.

Bainham, A. (1998b) *Children: The modern law* (2nd edition), Bristol: Family Law.

Barnett, A. (1998) *Contact and domestic violence – the ideological divide. Barristers' representation of women in child contact disputes where domestic violence is an issue*, London: Brunel University.

Buchanan, A. (1994) *Working in partnership under the Children Act 1989*, Aldershot: Avebury.

Buchanan, A. and Hudson, B. (2000) *Promoting children's emotional well-being*, Oxford: Oxford University Press.

Buchanan, A. and Ten Brinke, J.-A. (1997) *What happened when they were grown up? Outcomes from parenting experiences*, York: Joseph Rowntree Foundation.

Buchanan, A., Ten Brinke, J.-A. and Flouri, E. (forthcoming) *Emotional and behavioural problems in childhood and distress in adult life: Risk and protective factors*, Oxford: University of Oxford.

CAFCASS (Children and Family Court Advisory and Support Service) (2000) *'Children First': Setting up a unified Children and Family Court Advisory and Support Service*, London: CAFCASS.

Champion, L.A., Goodall, G. and Rutter, M. (1995) 'Behaviour problems in childhood and stressors in early adult life: a 20-year follow-up of London school children', *Psychological Medicine*, vol 25, no 2, pp 231-46.

Cherlin, A.J., Furstenberg, F.F., Chase-Lansdale, P.L., Kiernan, K.E., Robins, P.K., Morrison, D. and Teitler, J.G. (1991) 'Longitudinal studies of effects of divorce on children in Great Britain and the United States', *Science*, vol 252, no 2011, pp 1386-9.

Cheung, S.Y. and Buchanan, A. (1997) 'Malaise scores in adulthood of children and young people who have been in care', *Journal of Child Psychology and Psychiatry*, vol 38, no 5, pp 575-80.

Clisby, S., Cumming, Z., Davis, G., Dingwall, R., Fenn, P., Finch, S., Fitzgerald, R., Goldie, S., Greatbatch, D., James, A. and Pearce, J. (2000) *Monitoring publicly funded mediation*, London: Legal Services Commission.

Clulow, C. and Vincent, C. (1987) *In the child's best interests: Divorce court welfare and the search for a settlement*, London: Tavistock Publications.

Cretney, S. (1990) 'Foreword', in P. Monro and L. Forrester, *The guardian ad litem, law and practice*, Bristol: Family Law, p v.

Crockett, L.J., Eggebeen, D.J. and Hawkins, A.J. (1993) 'Fathers' presence and young children's behavioral and cognitive adjustment', *Journal of Family Issues*, vol 14, no 3, pp 355-77.

Davis, G. and Pearce, J. (1999) 'The welfare principle in action', *Family Law*, vol 28, pp 237-41.

Davis, G. (1997) Inaugural lecture, Faculty of Law, University of Bristol.

Davis, G. (2000) 'Love in a cold climate: disputes about children in the aftermath of parental separation', in S. Cretney (ed) *Family law: Essays for the new millennium*, London: Family Law, pp 127-42.

DoH (Department of Health) (1989) *An introduction to the Children Act 1989*, London: HMSO.

DoH (2000) *Framework for the assessment of children in need and their families*, London: DoH.

DoH (2001) *Children Act Report 1995-2000*, London: DoH.

DoH, Home Office, Lord Chancellor's Department and Welsh Office (1998) *Support services in family proceedings – Future organisation of court welfare services: consultation paper*, London: DoH.

Douglas, G., Butler, I., Murch, M., Robinson, M., and Scanlan, L. (in press) *Children's perspectives and experience of the divorce process*, Bristol: Family Law.

Douglas, G., Murch, M., Scanlon, L. and Perry, A. (2000) 'Safeguarding children's welfare in non-contentious divorce: towards a new conception of the legal process', *Modern Law Review*, vol 63, pp 177-96.

Elliott, B.J. and Richards, M. (1991) 'Children and divorce: educational performance and behaviour before and after parental separation', *International Journal of Law and the Family*, vol 5, pp 258-76.

Epstein, N.B. and Schlesinger, S.E. (2000) 'Couples in crisis', in F.M. Dattilio and A. Freeman (eds) *Cognitive-behavioural strategies in crisis intervention*, 2nd edn, New York, NY: The Guildford Press, pp 291-315.

Ferri, E. and Smith, K. (1996) *Parenting in the 1990s*, London/York: Family Policy Studies Centre/Joseph Rowntree Foundation.

Freeman, P. and Hunt, J. (1998) *Parental perspectives on care proceedings*, London: The Stationery Office.

Goldberg, D. and Williams, P. (1988) *A users guide to the general health questionnaire*, Windsor: NFER-Nelson.

Goldstein, J., Freud, A. and Solnit, A.J. (1973) *Before the best interests of the child*, New York, NY: The Free Press.

Goodman, R. (1997) 'The Strengths and Difficulties Questionnaire: a research note', *Journal of Child Psychology and Psychiatry*, vol 38, no 5, pp 581-6.

Goodman, R. (2001) 'Information about the Strengths and Difficulties Questionnaires', at www.sdqinfo.com.

Grych, J.H. and Fincham, F.D. (1999) 'The adjustment of children from divorced families: implications of empirical research for clinical intervention', in R.M. Galatzer-Levy and L. Kraus (eds) *The scientific basis of child custody decisions*, New York, NY: John Wiley & Sons, pp 96-119.

Hale, B. (1995) 'Foreword', in R. White, P. Carr and N. Lowe, *The Children Act in practice*, 2nd edn, Butterworth's, p v.

Halpern, D. (1995) 'Values, morals and modernity', in M. Rutter and D.J. Smith (eds) *Psychosocial disorders in young people*, Chichester: John Wiley & Sons.

Harrington, R. (1992) 'Annotation: the natural history and treatment of child and adolescent affective disorders', *Journal of Child Psychology and Psychiatry*, vol 33, no 8, pp 1287-302.

Harrington, R., Fudge, H., Rutter, M., Pickles, A. and Hill, J. (1990) 'Adult outcomes of childhood and adolescent depression', *Archives of General Psychiatry*, vol 47, no 5, pp 465-73.

Harwin, J., Owen, M., Locke, R. and Forrester, D. (forthcoming) *A study to investigate the implementation of care orders made under the Children Act 1989*.

Hawthorne, J., Richards, M. and Pryor, J. (in progress) 'Intervention and support services for children experiencing divorce and family change', University of Cambridge.

Health Advisory Service (1995) *Bridges over troubled waters*, London: HMSO.

Hester, M. and Radford, L. (1996) *Domestic violence and child contact arrangements in England and Denmark*, Bristol: The Policy Press.

Hetherington, E.M. and Stanley-Hagen, M. (1999) 'The adjustment of children with divorced parents: a risk and resiliency perspective', *Journal of Child Psychology and Psychiatry*, vol 40, no 1, pp 129-40.

Hetherington, E.M., Cox, M. and Cox, R. (1985) 'Long-term effects of divorce and remarriage on the adjustment of children', *Journal of the American Academy of Child Psychiatry*, vol 24, no 5, pp 518-30.

HM Inspectorate of Probation (1997) *Family court welfare work: Report of a thematic inspection*, London: Home Office.

Home Office (1994) *National standards for probation family court welfare work*, London: Home Office.

Home Office (1998) *Supporting families: A consultation document*, London: The Stationery Office.

Home Office (1999a) *The Stephen Lawrence Inquiry*, The Macpherson Report, London: The Stationery Office.

Home Office (1999b) *Living without fear*, London: The Stationery Office.

Home Office (2001) *Probation statistics: England and Wales 1999*, London: Home Office.

Hunt, J. (forthcoming) *Professionalising lay justice: The role of the court clerk in family proceedings*, London: Lord Chancellor's Department.

Hunt, J. (2000) 'Making and implementing timely decisions for children: research on a court sample', in A. Buchanan and B. Hudson (eds) *Promoting children's emotional well-being*, Oxford: Oxford University Press, pp 193-209.

Hunt, J. and Lawson, J. (1999) *Crossing the boundaries: The views of practitioners with experience of family court welfare and guardian ad litem work on the proposal to create a unified court welfare service*, Bristol: National Council for Family Proceedings.

Hunt, J., Macleod, A. and Thomas, C. (1999) *The last resort: Child protection, the courts and the 1989 Children Act*, London: The Stationery Office.

James, A. and Richards, M. (1999) 'Sociological perspectives, family policy, family law and children: adult thinking and sociological tinkering', *Journal of Social Welfare and Family Law*, vol 21, no 1, pp 23-39.

James, L.J. and Hay, W. (1992) *Court welfare work: Research practice and development*, Hull: University of Hull.

James, L.J. and Hay, W. (1993) *Court welfare in action*, Hemel Hempstead: Harvester Wheatsheaf.

Kaganas, F. (1999) 'Contact, conflict and risk', in S. Day Schlater (ed) *Undercurrents of divorce*, Aldershot: Ashgate, pp 99-120.

Kelly, J.B. (2000) 'Children's adjustment in conflicted marriage and divorce: a decade review of research', *Journal of the American Academy of Child and Adolescent Psychiatry*, vol 39, no 39, pp 963-73.

Kempe, R. and Kempe, C. (1978) *Child abuse*, Cambridge, MA: Harvard University Press.

King, M. (1987) 'Playing the symbols – custody and the Law Commission', *Family Law*, vol 17, pp 186-91.

King, M. and Piper, C. (1995) *How the law thinks about children*, 2nd edn, Aldershot: Arena.

Kohlberg, L., Ricks, D. and Snarey, J. (1984) 'Childhood development as a predictor of adaptation in adulthood', *Genetic Psychology Monographs*, vol 110, pp 91-172.

Kovacs, M. and Devlin, B. (1998) 'Internalizing disorders in childhood', *Journal of Child Psychology and Psychiatry*, vol 39, no 1, pp 47-63.

Kurki-Suonio, K. (2000) 'Joint custody as an interpretation of the best interests of the child', *International Journal of Law and the Family*, vol 14, no 3, pp 183-205.

Lamb, M.E. (1986) 'The changing role of fathers', in M.E. Lamb (ed) *The father's role: Applied perspectives*, New York, NY: John Wiley & Sons.

Lamb, M.E. (ed) (1999) *Parenting and child development in non-traditional families*, Mahwah, NJ: Erlbaum.

Law Commission (1988) *Report on guardianship and custody*, Law Commission Report No 172, London: Law Commission.

LCD (Lord Chancellor's Department) (2000a) *Judicial statistics 1999*, London: LCD.

LCD (2000b) *A report to the Lord Chancellor on the question of parental contact in cases where there is domestic violence*, London: LCD.

LCD (2000c) 'Setting up CAFCASS – progress report', website.

LCD (2001a) *Children and Family Court Advisory and Support Service (CAFCASS) Court Amendment Rules*, London: LCD.

LCD (2001b) *Making contact work: The facilitation of arrangements for contact between children and their non-residential parents; and the enforcement of court orders for contact*, London: LCD.

Lund, M. (1987) 'The non-custodial father: common challenges in parenting after divorce', in C. Lewis and M. O'Brien (eds) *Reassessing fatherhood*, Thousand Oaks, CA: Sage Publications.

Lyon, C. (1995) 'Representing children – towards 2000 and beyond', *Representing Children*, vol 8, no 2, pp 8-18.

Lyon, C., Surrey, E. and Timms, J. (1999) *Effective support services for children and young people when parental relationships break down*, National Youth Advocacy and the Gulbenkian Foundation.

Maclean, M. and Eekelaar, J. (1997) *The parental obligation: A study of parenthood across households*, Oxford: Hart Publishing.

Masson, J. and Winn-Oakley, M. (1999) *Out of hearing*, Chichester: John Wiley & Sons.

Moffitt, T.E. (1990) 'Juvenile delinquency and attention-deficit disorder: developmental trajectories from age three to fifteen', *Child Development*, vol 61, no 3, pp 893-910.

Murch, M. (1980) *Justice and welfare in divorce*, London: Sweet and Maxwell.

Murch, M., Hunt, J. and Macleod, A. (1990) *Representation of the child in civil proceedings research project 1985-89: Summary of conclusions and recommendations for the Department of Health*, Bristol: Socio-legal Centre for Family Studies, University of Bristol.

NFER-Nelson (2001) 'GHQ', at www.nfer-nelson.co.uk/ghq/index.htm.

O'Quigley, A. (1999) *Listening to children's views and representing their best interests: A summary of current research*, York: Joseph Rowntree Foundation.

Offord, D.R. and Bennett, K.J. (1994) 'Conduct disorder: long-term outcomes and intervention effectiveness', *Journal of American Academy of Adolescent Psychiatry*, vol 33, no 8, pp 1069-78.

Patterson, G.R., Dishion, T.J. and Chamberlain, P. (1993) 'Outcomes and methodological issues relating to treatment of antisocial children', in T.R. Giles (ed) *Handbook of effective psychotherapy*, New York, NY: Plenum Press, pp 43-88.

Pedro-Caroll, J.L. and Cowen, E.L. (1985) 'The children of divorce intervention program: an investigation of the efficiency of a school-based prevention programme', *Journal of Consulting and Clinical Psychology*, vol 14, pp 277-90.

Power, C., Manor, O. and Fox, J. (1991) *Health and class: The early years*, London: Chapman and Hall.

Radford, L., Sayer, S. and AMICA (1999) *Unreasonable fears? Child contact in the context of domestic violence*, Bristol: Women's Aid Federation of England.

Richards, M.P.M. and Dyson, C. (1982) *Separation, divorce and the development of children: A review for the Department of Health and Social Security by the Child Care and Development Group*, Cambridge: Cambridge University.

Rogers, B. and Pryor, J. (1998) *Divorce and separation: The outcomes for children*, York: Joseph Rowntree Foundation.

Salgo, L. (1998) 'Representing children in civil child protection proceedings – lessons from a comparative study of systems operating in the USA, Australia, France, Germany and England and Wales', *Representing Children*, vol 10, no 4, pp 225-37.

Sawyer, C. (1995) *The rise and fall of the third party*, Oxford: Centre for Socio-Legal Studies, University of Oxford.

Sawyer, C. (1999) *Rules, roles and relationships: The structure and function of child representation and welfare in family proceedings*, monograph, Oxford: Centre for Socio-Legal Studies, University of Oxford.

Scanlan, L., Perry, A. and Robinson, M. (2001) *Representing children*, vol 13, no 1, pp 34-47.

Scott, J., Braun, M. and Alwin, D. (1998) 'Partner, parent, worker: family and gender roles', in R. Jowell, J. Curtice, A. Park, L. Brode, K. Thomson and C. Bryson (eds) *British and European social attitudes: How Britain differs: the 15th report*, Aldershot: Ashgate.

Smart, C. and Neale, B. (1997) 'Arguments against virtue – must contact be enforced?', *Family Law*, vol 28, pp 232-6.

Spillane-Grieco, E. (2000) 'Cognitive-behavioural family therapy with a family in high-conflict divorce: a case study', *Clinical Social Work Journal*, vol 28, no 1, pp 105-19.

Sturge, C. and Glaser, D. (2000) *Family law*, vol 30, pp 615-29, September.

Timmis, G. (2000) 'The child first and foremost: creating a child-centred court service', MA dissertation, University of Westminster.

United Nations (1989) *Convention on the rights of the child*, New York, NY: United Nations.

Walker, J. (2001) *Information meetings and associated provisions within the Family Law Act 1996*, London: LCD.

Wallerstein, J.S. and Kelly, J.B. (1980) *Surviving the break-up: How children and parents cope with divorce*, London: Grant McIntyre.

Weiss, R.S. (1984) 'The impact of marital dissolution on income and consumption in single-parent households', *Journal of Marriage and the Family*, vol 46, pp 115-27.

White, R., Carr, P. and Lowe, N. (1995) *The Children Act in practice*, 2nd edn, London: Butterworth's.

Wiggins, R.D. and Bynner, J. (1993) 'Social attitudes', in E. Ferri (ed) *Life at 33*, London: National Children's Bureau, pp 162-83.

Table of cases

A v A (minors) (shared residence orders) [1995] 1 FCR 91 [1994] 1 FLR 669, CA.

Re A (contact: separate representation) [2001] 1 FLR 715.

A v N (committal: refusal of contact) [1997] 1 FLR 533 [1997] Fam Law 233 [1997] 2 FCR 475.

Re D (children) (shared residence orders) [2001] Fam Law 183 [2001] 1 FCR 147 [2000] 1 FLR 495.

Re H (minors) (access) [1992] 1 FLR 148 [1992] Fam Law 152.

Re H (contact: domestic violence) [2000] 2 FLR 334, CA.

Re J (a minor) (contact) [1994] 1 FLR 729, CA.

Re L (a child) (contact: domestic violence) [2000] 2 FCR 404 [2000] 4 All ER 609 [2000] 2 FLR 334, CA.

M v M (child access) [1973] 2 All ER 81, DC.

Re O (contact: imposition of conditions [1995] 2 FLR 124, CA.

Re M (contact: domestic violence)

Re V (contact: domestic violence)

Key: All ER *All England Law Reports*; CA Court of Appeal; DC District Court; Fam Law *Family Law*; FCR *Family Court Reports*; FLR *Family Law Reports*.

Useful websites

CAFCASS
www.cafcass.gov.uk

Lord Chancellor's Department, 'Family and individual matters'
www.lcd.gov.uk/family/famfr.htm

Home Office, 'Family'
www.homeoffice.gov.uk/new_indexs index_family.htm

Information on SDQ
www.sdqinfo.com

Information on GHQ
www.nfer-nelson.co.uk/ghq/index.htm

Appendix A:
How the research was undertaken

The research took place over a two-year period, March 1999 to February 2001. Figure A.1 gives an overview of the design of the research. The first parental interviews took place in May to December 1999, the second in May to November 2000. Children's interviews took place in July to October 2000.

Figure A.1: Overview of research design

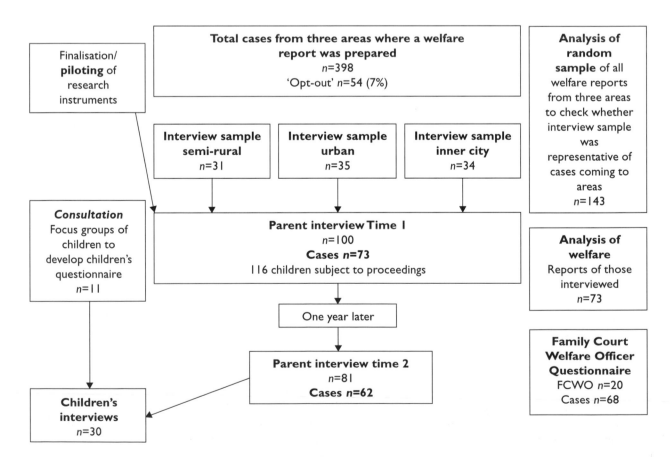

The key objectives of the research

1. *To find out from children aged eight and older:*
   - how they perceived the preparation of their welfare report and how they experienced the court's involvement in their parents' disputes;
   - whether they considered that their views were appropriately taken into account in the decision-making process;
   - their views on the arrangements made and any subsequent changes;
   - in what ways, if any, the process needs to be improved.

2. *To find out from parents:*
   - their views on the preparation of the welfare report, its place in the decision-making process and their level of satisfaction with the process and outcome of proceedings;
   - the degree to which decisions made in the court proceedings have been implemented or changed, the reasons for any changes and the impact on their children;
   - their views on improving the process.

3. *To assess any changes in the level of conflict* within the family, and the well-being of children and parents.

4. *To identify factors in the reporting and court process* which may contribute to a reduction in conflict and the promotion of the child's welfare.

The sample

As demonstrated by James and Hay (1992), family court welfare practice can differ considerably between areas. Three services were chosen for the study: an inner-city, an urban and a rural service.

The interview sample was drawn from a pool of 398 families on whom a welfare report was completed over a six-month period in 1999. All parents were initially contacted by the FCWS. Only 7% declined to take part. From the remaining cases the *interview sample* was matched to the sampling pool by the status of the applicant (mother/father, resident/non-resident), nature of application (contact, residence, contact and residence) and the ethnicity of the

parents (black, white, Asian, other; see Appendix B for a discussion of grouping issues).

A total of 100 parents (in 73 cases) were first interviewed soon after the order had been made and 81 parents (in 62 cases) were interviewed again approximately 12 months later. The major reason for sample attrition between the two stages was parents who had moved or could not be contacted.

Both interviews with parents involved a semi-structured questionnaire. Most interviews were tape-recorded. The possibility of interviewing children over the age of eight was broached with parents at first interview and permission sought at the second.

A total of 30 children were interviewed individually by the research team. Less than 10% of those approached refused to take part. The content of the children's interviews was informed by focus groups of children attending two contact centres in the south of England in which 11 children were involved. The children's interviews were also informed by the work undertaken by Douglas et al (in press).

Welfare reports were seen in all cases and a sample of FCWOs responded to a questionnaire. Figure A.1 illustrates the research design.

The representativeness of the sample

The study was designed to ensure that the interview sample was as representative as possible of cases coming to the study areas. There was concern, however, that those parents agreeing to be interviewed may have been, in some way, a particular group which would have biased the findings. Accordingly, once the sample had been collected there were two opportunities to check on its representativeness. The first involved examining a *random selection of 143 welfare reports* of cases that were not involved in the study but that had been completed during the same period. When these welfare reports were compared with the interview sample, it was found that the interview sample was well matched on the key criteria and the extent of domestic violence, but may have underestimated the extent of cases involving more serious child protection concerns.

The second check on the representativeness of those interviewed arose by asking the FCWOs who had prepared the welfare report on the sample cases how these compared, on a number of key dimensions, to others they had handled. Information was obtained in 44 cases. FCWOs indicated that they were within the average range in terms of their level of difficulty and complexity.

Standardised measures to assess well-being

Two well-validated measures were used to assess emotional well-being in parents and children. The 12-question version of the General Health Questionnaire (GHQ) (Goldberg and Williams, 1988) was used to assess parental well-being, and the Strengths and Difficulties Questionnaire (SDQ) (Goodman, 1997; parent-report and child-report versions) to measure the children's levels of distress. The Goodman SDQ is extensively used to give a broad indication of child well-being. Further details of both the GHQ and the SDQ are given in Chapter 8.

Statistical analyses

At the time of the first interviews (time 1) the study frequencies are presented as percentages either of cases (73) or of the parents interviewed (100). In reporting time 2 findings (from the second interviews) a similar practice is adopted. The numbers involved are given in the title of each figure. In Chapter 7 on the children's views, raw numbers are given because the findings are more tentative and only 30 children were interviewed. Owing to the small numbers, tests of statistical significance are omitted from this publication.

Showing the direction of satisfaction with the process

When early drafts of our findings were shown to the research Advisory Group and colleagues, there was a request that, although we could not demonstrate statistical significance between different groups, it would be helpful to compare the general direction of

satisfaction with the process at different stages between groups. For example, how did *fathers* feel about the process compared to *mothers*? How did mothers who had experienced *domestic violence* fare compared to those who did not? Did it make any difference if parents were *applicants* or *respondents*? Was there a difference between those receiving *legal aid* and those *not receiving legal aid*? Were the outcomes different depending on whether they were served by a family court in an *inner-city*, *urban* or *rural* area? Since the study involved 40% of cases in which one or both parents were from an *ethnic minority group*, did their levels of satisfaction differ from those of *white* parents? Were those who returned to court for *a second or further time* more or less satisfied than those who came to the court *for the first time*? Accordingly the following key groups were selected:

Key groups

- Father applicant non-resident parent/mother respondent resident parent (most applicants were non-resident fathers and most respondents were non-resident mothers).
- Inner-city/urban/rural FCWSs.
- Parents previously married/not married.
- On Income Support/not on Income Support.
- On legal aid/not on legal aid.
- Fear at the start of the proceedings (mothers only)/no fear.
- Ethnicity: black/white (see Appendix B).
- Ligitant type: first timer to proceedings/not first timer to proceedings (see Chapter 2 for definition).
- Parental emotional health: high score GHQ (above threshold indicating a departure from normal functioning and a significant level of distress)/low score (below threshold).
- Child emotional health (parent-report): abnormal or borderline SDQ scores/normal score.

Initially, three outcomes indicating satisfaction at different stages of the process were selected. A fourth indicator on the parents' attitude to the ordering of the welfare report was added as a comparison to the other three.

> ## Indicators of satisfaction at different stages of the process (parent interview)
>
> - Reaction to outcomes of court proceedings: 'entirely positive'.
> - Satisfaction with the preparation of the welfare report: 'satisfied' and 'mainly satisfied'.
> - 12 months later, satisfaction with the preparation of the welfare report: 'completely or mainly satisfied'.
> - Added as a comparison: attitude to the ordering of the welfare report: 'positive'.

In Chapter 10 the first three measures were brought together to give an overall picture on the general direction of satisfaction between different groups over the whole process.

B

Appendix B: Ethnic identity and religion of the sample

Parents were asked to describe their ethnic identity. The descriptions are reproduced in full in Table B.1. The sample was highly diverse in terms of the parents' self-reported nationality or ethnic background and religion. Although 30% of the parents interviewed came from minority ethnic backgrounds, because of the small numbers involved in the subgroups it was not possible to analyse parents' responses according to their ethnic or religious background. As discussed earlier, the only way to generate large enough numbers to make meaningful comparison possible was by grouping parents into those who broadly fell into the black population and those who broadly fell into the white population. It was recognised that this was a limitation of the study.

Table B.1: Ethnic identity of parents

Ethnic identity	Number of parents
African	2
African-Caribbean	2
African-European	1
Anglicised Asian	1
Anglo-Indian	1
Arabic American	1
Asian	1
Black African American	1
Black British	2
Black British/African-Caribbean	1
Brazilian	1
British Asian	1
Chinese	1
English/Spanish	1
English/St Lucian	1
Ethiopian	1
Indian subcontinent	7
Japanese	1
Kenyan Asian	1
Sierra Leone	1
South American	1
West Indian	1
White, Canadian	1
White, Dutch	1
White, Irish	1
White, other	4
White, Spanish	1
White, UK	60
Zairian	1

Parents were also asked to describe their religion. Their answers are reproduced in Table B.2.

Table B.2: Religion of parents

Religion	Number of parents
Buddhist	1
Christian (mainstream)	46
Christian (sect)	5
Hindu	3
Muslim	2
Sikh	4
Other	5
None	31
Missing data	3

Appendix C:
Assessment tools
used in the study

Questionnaires

In assessing the child's well-being, both the parent-report and the child-report version of the Goodman Strengths and Difficulties Questionnaire (SDQ) (Goodman, 1997, 2001) proved useful in giving an objective measurement of child well-being which could be compared to children in the general population. The SDQ is readily available from the Department of Health (DoH): 'Family Pack of Questionnaires and Scales' in the materials for the *Framework for the assessment of children in need and their families* (DoH, 2000). The General Health Questionnaire (GHQ) (12-question version) (Goldberg and Williams, 1988; NFER-Nelson, 2001) is a useful tool for measuring parental well-being. This is available from NFER Windsor; there is a cost for using it.

The children's quiz

In this study, 'the children's quiz' was developed from ideas given by the children in the contact centres and questions used by the Douglas et al study (in press). The aim was to develop a short tool that would, in a non-threatening way, assess children's relationships with their parents and the effects of parental conflict. The tool proved very effective when used with the 30 children who were interviewed. Older children can complete the questionnaire independently; younger children may need the questions read out before selecting their response. The possible answers are displayed next to the question and the child circles the one that they choose. This tool needs further development. CAFCASS officers are very

welcome to photocopy it and see how it works for them.

Various questions on the same theme can be grouped together and the score used to elucidate the child's views on their relationship with their father, relationship with their mother, and conflict and arguing. Reliability analyses (in brackets) for these 'subscales' are shown below.

Relationship with father

Questions: 9, 10, 16, 19, 21, 34
(Cronbach's Alpha = 0.67)

Relationship with mother

Questions: 5, 12, 22, 27, 31, 33
(Cronbach's Alpha = 0.71)

Conflict/arguing

Questions: 8, 11, 13, 14, 17, 18, 20, 23, 24, 25, 30, 32
(Cronbach's Alpha = 0.74)

Possible answers	Scoring for 'subscales' ★ = reverse scoring
True	1
Sort of true	2
Not true	3
Don't know	No score

The children's quiz

Here are some things that children and young people think and feel when their parents do not live together.

You can choose:

T	if the item is true for you
ST	if the item is sort of true
NT	if the item is false
DK	if you don't know the answer or it is not relevant to your situation

All you have to do is circle the answer that is true for you. There are no right or wrong answers.

Let's give it a try: I like reading

    T   **ST**   **NT**   **DK**

Do you agree?

1.	My parents are happier when I'm with them than when I'm not	T	ST	NT	DK
2.	It would upset me if other kids asked a lot of questions about my parents*	T	ST	NT	DK
3.	I would like to get to know my dad better	T	ST	NT	DK
4.	I feel that my parents still love me	T	ST	NT	DK
5.	My mum and I get on really well	T	ST	NT	DK
6.	I find it difficult to tell my parents what I really want*	T	ST	NT	DK
7.	I would like to get to know my mum better	T	ST	NT	DK
8	My mum says critical things about my dad when I'm with her*	T	ST	NT	DK
9.	My dad and I get on really well	T	ST	NT	DK
10.	What ever worries my dad has, I know that it is Ok for me to talk to him about things that bother me	T	ST	NT	DK
11.	My dad says critical things about my mum when I'm with him*	T	ST	NT	DK
12.	My mum is interested in how I do at school	T	ST	NT	DK
13.	My mum makes me feel guilty for wanting to spend time with my dad*	T	ST	NT	DK
14.	My dad makes me feel guilty for wanting to spend time with my mum*	T	ST	NT	DK
15.	Sometimes worries about my family get in the way of schoolwork*	T	ST	NT	DK
16.	My dad is interested in how I do at school	T	ST	NT	DK
17.	My parents agree about how much time I can spend with each of them	T	ST	NT	DK
18.	My mum and dad often disagree about when and how long I should visit*	T	ST	NT	DK
19.	I usually have a good time when I'm with my dad	T	ST	NT	DK
20.	I never see my parents arguing or disagreeing	T	ST	NT	DK
21.	I'm scared of my dad*	T	ST	NT	DK
22.	I usually have a good time when I'm with mum	T	ST	NT	DK
23.	When my parents have an argument they shout at each other*	T	ST	NT	DK
24.	My parents have pushed or shoved each other during an argument*	T	ST	NT	DK
25.	If it would mean an end to the arguments, I would rather not see mum/dad*	T	ST	NT	DK
26.	I would like to spend more time with my dad	T	ST	NT	DK
27.	I'm scared of my mum*	T	ST	NT	DK
28.	Sometimes I am so worried about my family that I stay awake at night	T	ST	NT	DK
29.	I would like to spend more time with my mum	T	ST	NT	DK
30.	Whatever worries my parents have, it does not interfere with my schoolwork	T	ST	NT	DK
31.	Spending time with mum interferes with what I want to do at the weekend*	T	ST	NT	DK
32.	I tell mum/dad when I want to see them and they go along with it	T	ST	NT	DK
33.	Whatever worries my mum has I know it is OK for me to talk to her about things that bother me	T	ST	NT	DK
34.	Spending time with dad interferes with what I want to do at the weekend*	T	ST	NT	DK
35.	I have lots of good friends to whom I can talk to about my family	T	ST	NT	DK

Very good ... you're doing well!